"With grace and honesty, Tara Beth Lea... ... coming a woman senior pastor in a prominent evangelical church. In doing so, she blazes a trail for us all, both men and women, in empowering women for ministry. Robust in its theology, practical in its wisdom, *Emboldened* tells us why God's mission demands nothing less of us in these times: women *and* men together leading God's church."
David Fitch, Northern Seminary, author of *Faithful Presence*

"A double shot of spiritual espresso to awaken, encourage, and embolden every woman in the kingdom of God."
Frank Viola, author of *From Eternity to Here* and *God's Favorite Place on Earth*

"It's time for the church to expand its imagination to include the strengths that women bring to the table as senior leaders, and Tara Beth Leach helps us do just that in this engaging book. Finally we have a primer for women in pastoral ministry that is both practical and theological. *Emboldened* is unflinching in naming the challenges that keep women sidelined in the church while at the same time inspiring those willing to brave those challenges. This will be the first book I recommend to women considering vocational ministry."
Gail Wallace, cofounder, The Junia Project

"One day, Lord willing, the American church will look back in disbelief at our failure to see the emboldening of women as essential to living faithfully under the rule and reign of God. This book, however, presents the opportunity to bring us much nearer to that day. I commend it strongly to all, but especially to my fellow brothers in Christ; may we heed this vision as a fresh, kingdom-oriented call to 'biblical manhood.'"
JR Rozko, codirector, Missio Alliance

"Pastor Tara Beth Leach has produced an inspiring writing to embolden those who are called for ministry. For women called to vocational ministry the pathway is not easy, but Leach reminds us that the call cannot be ignored. This is the mission of God, and in the words of Pastor Tara Beth, 'I get to do this.' This book is a vital new resource for the church. It's for all women who are called to ministry and for those who will embolden others who have been called."
Carla Sunberg, general superintendent, Church of the Nazarene

"*Emboldened* is a clarion call of instruction and inspiration to not settle for fifty percent participation, but for the church to engage one hundred percent of its people in the mission. My friend Tara Beth Leach is an important young voice that offers the church of Jesus a much better vision of the future. If you want to be challenged, inspired, or catch a glimpse of the church's tomorrow, read *Emboldened*."

Dave Ferguson, visionary leader of NewThing, author of *Finding Your Way Back to God* and *Starting Over*

"We both believe that if we are to be the transformational movement that Jesus intended us to be, we are going to have to activate the God-given agency of women in the organized church and beyond. Until that happens, the body of Christ will continue to limp along. Tara Beth's new book is a loving invitation for the church to take women seriously enough to empower them for the frontline of leadership and mission. Viva!"

Deb Hirsch and Alan Hirsch, authors and leaders in the missional church movement

"Tara Beth Leach perfectly articulates the ache I feel for the day when the church will embolden men and women to serve God in all spheres of ministry without gender qualifiers. It's a passionate call for revolutionary change in our churches, but it's also a warmly written guide, full of very practical advice, useful steps, and stories to sustain you in that journey. Please read this book. Please."

Michael Frost, Morling College, Sydney

"Over the years, I've heard the keepers of patriarchy shriek and howl over the imagined ills of what they deem the 'feminization of the church.' But if the 'feminization of the church' means more pastors like Tara Beth Leach, I'm all for it! I fervently hope that *Emboldened* will help pave the way for many more women in pastoral ministry."

Brian Zahnd, lead pastor, Word of Life Church, St. Joseph, Missouri, author of *Sinners in the Hands of a Loving God*

"Women who are called to ministry need a pastor—to tell them they're not alone, that they can do this. They need a voice to speak truth over their calling and identity. In Tara Beth Leach they find such a voice. Her warm, pastoral authority twice blesses her readers, both as recipients of her care and as they watch her model what ministry can be."

Mandy Smith, pastor, author of *The Vulnerable Pastor*

"*Emboldened* is the book you need to give to every woman who is called into ministry. Thorough, hopeful, pragmatic, and bold, I hope it becomes required reading for every student of Scripture and discipleship because this is equal parts roadmap and encouragement. Tara Beth has given us the missing piece of the puzzle for churches who want to empower women to lead and step out in faithfulness to their calling and giftedness for the sake of the gospel."

Sarah Bessey, author of *Jesus Feminist* and *Out of Sorts: Making Peace with an Evolving Faith*

"It's easy for a church to say they affirm women in ministry. It's much harder, as gifted and called women know all too well, to be a church that actually equips and empowers women to be who God created and called them to be. With pastoral wisdom, Tara Beth Leach encourages women who have been sidelined by churches who made promises that remain unkept. With prophetic vision, she illustrates a path forward for these churches that we might practice what we preach. And she does it all by weaving her own story—told with raw vulnerability—into the story of Scripture and the story of the church, which has from the beginning been shaped by the voices of our spiritual mothers as much as our spiritual fathers. She offers this as a precious gift to all of us, men and women, that the church of Jesus might more perfectly show the world what it looks like when God's kingdom comes here on earth as it is in heaven."

JR. Forasteros, pastor, author of *Empathy for the Devil*

"Very few issues are as potentially divisive and hurtful as the gender issue for leaders, teachers, and pastors in the local church. The pathway for many has been lonely and discouraging. Tara Beth Leach steps into this hard place with a strong, wise, and gracious voice. This book is an enormous gift to men and women trying to figure out how to honor God and one another in the ways we guide, shape, and care for the bride of Christ. I can't wait to share this book to embolden the leaders I'm coaching!"

Nancy Beach, leadership coach, Slingshot Group, author of *Gifted to Lead*

EMBOLDENED

A VISION FOR

EMPOWERING WOMEN

IN MINISTRY

TARA BETH LEACH

FOREWORD BY SCOT McKNIGHT

IVP Books

An imprint of InterVarsity Press
Downers Grove, Illinois

InterVarsity Press
P.O. Box 1400, Downers Grove, IL 60515-1426
ivpress.com
email@ivpress.com

InterVarsity Press® is the book-publishing division of InterVarsity Christian Fellowship/USA®, a movement of students and faculty active on campus at hundreds of universities, colleges, and schools of nursing in the United States of America, and a member movement of the International Fellowship of Evangelical Students. For information about local and regional activities, visit intervarsity.org.

All Scripture quotations, unless otherwise indicated, are taken from The Holy Bible, New International Version®, NIV®. Copyright © 1973, 1978, 1984, 2011 by Biblica, Inc.™ Used by permission of Zondervan. All rights reserved worldwide. www.zondervan.com The "NIV" and "New International Version" are trademarks registered in the United States Patent and Trademark Office by Biblica, Inc.™

Excerpts from Missio blog posts, Missio Alliance, used by permission.

Excerpt from Tara Beth Leach, "The Symphonic Melody: Wesleyan Holiness Theology Meets New Perspective Paul," in The Apostle Paul and the Christian Life, ed. Scot McKnight and Joe Modica (Baker Academic, a division of Baker Publishing Group: 2016), used by permission.

Excerpts from Tara Beth Leach, "I Don't Fit the Senior Pastor Mold," Christianity Today, September 12, 2016, used by permission.

While any stories in this book are true, some names and identifying information may have been changed to protect the privacy of individuals.

Cover design: David Fassett
Interior design: Daniel van Loon
Images: © OttoKrause / iStockphoto

ISBN 978-0-8308-4524-8 (print)
ISBN 978-0-8308-8758-3 (digital)

Printed in the United States of America ♾

InterVarsity Press is committed to ecological stewardship and to the conservation of natural resources in all our operations. This book was printed using sustainably sourced paper.

Library of Congress Cataloging-in-Publication Data

A catalog record for this book is available from the Library of Congress.

P	22	21	20	19	18	17	16	15	14	13	12	11	10	9	8	7	6	5	4	3	2	1
Y	35	34	33	32	31	30	29	28	27	26	25	24	23	22	21	20	19	18	17			

For Jeff.

My love, my partner, and the one who

emboldens me to ministry every day.

CONTENTS

FOREWORD

Scot McKnight

IN MY FIRST TERM AS A PROFESSOR at Northern Seminary
was a young woman, Tara Beth Leach. She was clearly engaged
in every topic and wrote papers that captured my interest because they not only examined the Bible carefully but showed
the implications of her papers for the church. I had Tara Beth
in a few more classes, and her work was such that I then asked
her to be my graduate assistant. Kris (my wife) and I have
walked with and prayed for Tara Beth over every one of her
moves in the last five years, but her recent move to pastor First
Church of the Nazarene in Pasadena revealed the giftedness
Tara Beth has. When she preaches and when she leads, she is
doing what God has called her to do.

Over four years at Northern Seminary we had many conversations about women in ministry and how best to embolden
gifted women in their ministries, and one of our discussions led
to this: avoid *justice*, emphasize *giftedness*. So many have an instinct to turn the discussion about what the Bible teaches about
women and ministry into a fight, and the first card laid on the
table is *justice*. For many it expresses something profoundly
deep, but for church folks it sounds like politics and culture

wars. I myself do believe silencing the voice of women is an injustice, but not just to women: it is an injustice to what the Bible actually says, and therefore it is an injustice to the women God has gifted. But instead of pulling that argument out of the bag, it is far wiser, far less inflammatory, and far more compelling for a woman to teach or preach or exercise her gift. Justice will become obvious when the woman's gifting is obvious.

Another of our discussions prompted this observation: males on the platform need to slide over and give women a place. It's a fact today that males are in power (define that term in positive or even negative ways, but power is at work) and for gifted women to exercise their gifts requires the permission of males. Yes, that's exactly what I mean: males are on the platform, and the only way for a woman to gain access is for males to move over. *Cruciform*—a word that tumbles off Tara Beth's tongue often—leadership requires males to surrender their power to anyone gifted, including women. Perhaps this foreword can encourage males in power to consider how they might make room for women on the platform. Power in the hands of a cruciform leader becomes transformative power. Instead of exercising authority over someone or creating hierarchical structures, cruciform power emboldens others.

Once a denominational leader told me he couldn't relate to a chapter I had written because every story in the chapter was about a woman. I gulped, took a deep breath, and tried to avoid blurting out the obvious, but this was the question: How do you think women feel almost every Sunday in most evangelical churches? The stories male pastors tell are far more often about males, and if that denominational leader would hold up

the mirror he might see that stories about women are nec-
essary too. How can young, gifted women know there is a place
for them on the platform if they don't hear stories about
women ministering? Tara Beth tells stories of women, and the
stories of women will provide for readers of *Emboldened* examples of women exercising their gifts.

Tara Beth and I agree 100 percent on the most important
topic of conversation: What did women do? That is, instead of
narrowing our debates to some restricting texts in the New
Testament—like 1 Timothy 2:8-15—and fighting over the
meaning of words and the confinement of women, why not
turn our attention to texts in the whole Bible to see what
women did in the Bible? Surely Paul's words in 1 Timothy will
not undercut what women had done, what women were doing
in his own mission in his own day, and what women would be
gifted to do! What we find is women ruling and judging and
leading and prophesying and discerning and announcing and
teaching and being apostles and deacons.

Those women did what they did because they were emboldened by the Spirit of God and the church's reception of the
Spirit's gifting. Tara Beth has chosen the right word to describe
not only women who have gone before us and what God is
doing among women today, but also what church leaders especially need to be doing today: emboldening women as a way of
letting the gifts of God be given to the people of God.

As Tara Beth's former teacher and as a representative of
Northern Seminary, we are all proud of her. Not because she's
gone where few have gone but because she has received the
gifts of God and is using them for God's glory.

INTRODUCTION

A Burden for the Church

PASTORS SURROUNDED HER AS SHE KNELT with her head bowed. It was another ordination ceremony for a handful of pastors in our denomination's district, but this one hit me differently. With my hands on her shoulders, dozens of pastors prayed for her, and one pastor prayed a prayer of blessing, commissioning, and anointing. I wept.

It wasn't that I wasn't grateful; no, not that. No one was arguing over the biblical and theological grounds for her ordination; no, it was a celebration. No one was resisting or protesting; no, it was an affirmation. I was grateful she was being ordained—after all, many denominations don't ordain women! But as we gathered around this soon-to-be-commissioned ordained pastor, I was overcome with emotion for the seemingly invisible resistance she might one day encounter. Would she find a pulpit to preach in? Would she find a place to serve? Would she be given a platform to lead from? Would she be welcomed to the table with her male counterparts? Will her voice be heard in meetings? Will she have to defend her calling? As we commissioned her I wondered what she might encounter.

So in that moment, I prayed through my tears. I prayed that she would be a woman emboldened by the Spirit of the living God to proclaim the good news in all things, and I prayed that her brothers in Christ would empower her to be a colaborer, and I prayed that the bride of Christ would boldly name and resist the systems and barriers that keep women sidelined.

I write this book as a grateful woman, but also as a burdened woman. Although many women enroll in seminaries and reach ordination, many still find themselves pushed to the side with no place to serve. I have sat and prayed with countless women who have been pushed aside or have been silenced or feel invisible within their own congregations and Christian organizations. For some, it's too late—they've already walked away. Others are hanging on by a thread, and some have pushed through. There are success stories, no doubt, but still not enough. The church can do better.

Over the years I have noticed something in many *well-meaning, Spirit-filled* churches. To put it bluntly, women are marginalized and are left without opportunities to harness and use their God-given gifts to the fullest simply because of their gender. Although many churches affirm women in ministry, these same communities sometimes have no idea how to *embolden* women in their midst as men continue to saturate the leadership structures. Women who are gifted to teach, preach, lead, evangelize, and shepherd are all too often sidelined. The body of Christ is disjointed—privileged men are soaring in their gifts, and women are *still* silenced. This status quo will continue indefinitely until men and women partner together in this great mission we have been called to.

On Sunday mornings, I often look around the congregation and wonder how many women sitting in the pews have lost the kingdom imagination for their role in the body of Christ. I sometimes wonder how different the worldwide church would be if all the women in the pews lived into their full potential of using their gifts to edify the body of Christ. How many women have extraordinary gifts of leadership but are held back because only the men in their congregations are given opportunities to lead? How many women have supernatural gifts of preaching and teaching but don't know it because they have bought into the narrative that men alone preach and teach? How many women have unusual gifts of shepherding but are blind to it because they've never observed a woman shepherd?

Not too long ago I came across some statistics for the Church of the Nazarene—a denomination that has affirmed women in ministry since its inception.[1] These statistics exposed a troublesome phenomenon. When the report was released, women made up nearly 20 percent of active clergy. However, only 14 percent of clergy women were senior pastors—less than 3 percent of all senior pastorates. Additionally, a higher percentage of women (19.3 percent) were not assigned at all.[2] Sadly, these statistics reflect the landscape for many women in ministry. In another study through Barna, it was found that women are frustrated by the lack of opportunities in their local church and even believe they are undervalued by their church leaders. As many as 20 percent feel underutilized, and 16 percent feel they are limited by their gender.[3] The study notes that although these seem like small percentages, this actually amounts to millions of women in the United States who feel sidelined in their churches.

After reading these statistics, I wanted to commiserate with some of my sisters in Christ. As I sat at my computer, I could see all of the faces of women who have left the ministry *because it was just too hard*. I could see the faces of women in ministry who have been deeply wounded by the church, those who have given up altogether, or those who, although they have a gift to preach, have no pulpit to preach from, or the ones who no longer see the stress as something worth pressing through.

Since 2004, I have served in both parachurch ministry and pastoral ministry in local churches as a youth pastor, women's pastor, a teaching pastor, and now a senior pastor. Every Sunday I stand before a congregation that affirms all of me and also emboldens me. They've given me a place to lead, teach, preach, and shepherd. I am grateful for every opportunity, review all of my years with great fondness, and look ahead to the future with much excitement. I rejoice when I have the opportunity to share the story of God—the life, teachings, fulfillment, death, resurrection, and ascension of Jesus, my King. I can do nothing but shed tears of joy when someone first decides to turn their heart and life to Jesus. I delight when I watch the people within the body of Christ discover the gifts and talents God has given them through the Spirit. I become weak in the knees when someone in our midst begins to read the Bible, saturate in its words, and become a student of the Word.

I desperately love the church. Sometimes I stand in utter disbelief that not only did God call me to teach and preach, but I *actually get to do it.* I am grateful for the men and women who have emboldened me to stand behind the pulpit and teach in a way that only Tara Beth in the Spirit could. I am grateful for congregations who have believed in me and loved me, and I am grateful for a congregation that loves me now.

But also, as a woman who has been in full-time ministry for over a decade, I understand wounds—I know them intimately. There have been days that I too have wanted to give up. There have been moments when the pressure of ministry and the obstacles as a woman are so challenging that I think, *why bother?* With two little boys at home, I often think it would be easier to walk away from the ministry. But I haven't, and I won't. I'm in for the long haul, and I want other women to join me. I want to pull all of the wounded women into one big room and tell them to *keep on preaching on.* I want to tell them to not give up, to come back to the church, to persevere together, and to hold fast to the One who calls us.

And I can see the faces of every little girl, every young seminarian, and every young and aspiring minister. I want to write them a love letter and show them the kingdom vision for women in the body of Christ. I want to offer them words of hope, inspiration, and encouragement, so that when they reach bumps in the road, they would know Whose they are and by Whom they've been called.

But I also want to pull into a room all of the male pastors and church leaders who are professing egalitarians. I want to hold a town hall meeting of sorts and give *them* a pep talk, and plainly teach them how to embolden women in ministry and give them a platform to flourish. Far too many women have been left without wings to soar, pulpits to preach, and churches to serve.

It is my prayer that women will read this book and be inspired to use their gifts for the edification of the kingdom and the glory of God, and men will walk away with practical steps on *how* to embolden women in their midst. This book is for men and women who already understand the biblical and theological account for the full inclusion of women in church leadership.

If you're looking for an extensive theological and hermeneutical exposé on why women of the Bible were emboldened and why women today are called to serve alongside their brothers, you won't find that here. This is not *that* book. Many wonderful books have made important biblical and theological arguments *for* women in ministry.[4] Instead, women will be able to read this book and be inspired to use their gifts for the edification of the kingdom and the glory of God, and men will walk away with practical steps on *how* to embolden women in their church. It is also my hope that women who don't necessarily want to be in full-time ministry but want to use their gifts faithfully within the body of Christ (including but not limited to Bible study leaders, small group leaders, board members, campus ministers, evangelists, writers, professors, worship leaders, and Sunday school teachers) will also find encouragement in this book and then reclaim the kingdom vision for women in the church.

There might be a number of reasons you picked up this book. Maybe you are a young woman who has experienced a new call to ministry, or maybe you are a young seminarian preparing to enter full-time ministry. No matter who you are, I hope these stories bring you hope. I believe in Holy Spirit leadings and promptings, and I believe in angelic nudges, so perhaps the Spirit has led you to this book. Whether you're a woman who is at the end of your rope and is ready to walk away from ministry, or you're a male pastor scratching your head wondering how to better embolden women in your midst, I pray that this book not only blesses and encourages you, but also opens your eyes to God's heart for the church.

A prayer for you, the reader:

Lord, I thank you so much for this reader. I thank you for the leading of your Spirit to not only write this book, but I also thank you for leading the reader to pick up this book. I pray for the reader because I so desperately believe in the messages and stories that will unfold in this book, I believe that it is your heart for the church. Before us is a new frontier for women and men in the church, and I thank you for the countless women that have already paved the way to bring us to this point. I pray that you would inspire within *this reader* to see the church *anew* and *fresh* through your eyes. I pray that as the reader flips through the pages of this book their heart would be open and moldable to your wise counsel. Lord, embolden us all, men and women, to serve alongside of one another with a holy passion for your work. Amen.

PART 1

EM**BOLD**ENED
WOMEN

ONE

THIS IS OUR STORY

AROUND AD 33. As she sobbed, the tears rolled down her face. He was gone, nowhere to be found. Mary Magdalene stooped low to peer into the tomb. Days before, she stood at the foot of the cross as her Lord suffered. Keyed in on every movement, every word, every breath, every emotion, she watched. Tall above her, head down, he suffered—and she watched.[1]

And as he was wrapped up and laid in the tomb, Mary watched. He was, after all, her Lord, her Savior, her teacher, her love. And now it was over. The bitter end had now come and gone.

Longing to capture a glimpse of her Lord, hoping that maybe his body wasn't taken after all, she peered in. Imagine the utter shock she must have felt to see two angels sitting where Jesus had been lying.

They asked her, "Woman, why are you crying?"

"They have taken my Lord away," she said, "and I don't know where they have put him." At this, she turned around and saw Jesus standing there, but she did not realize that it was Jesus.

He asked her, "Woman, why are you crying? Who is it you are looking for?"

Thinking he was the gardener, she said, "Sir, if you have carried him away, tell me where you have put him, and I will get him."

Jesus said to her, "Mary."

She turned toward him and cried out in Aramaic, "Rabboni!" (which means "Teacher").

Jesus said, "Do not hold on to me, for I have not yet ascended to the Father." (Jn 20:13-17)

As Mary's bitter sorrow and hopelessness shift to joy at the vision of her Lord and Savior, Jesus *sees* Mary. Jesus *sees Mary*; Jesus *affirms* Mary's role; Jesus recognizes her intrinsic value as a minister; Jesus *emboldens* Mary to be the first to preach the tidings of the resurrection. The risen Lord, King Jesus, sends Mary:

> "Go . . . to my brothers and tell them, 'I am ascending to my Father and your Father, to my God and your God.'"
>
> Mary Magdalene went to the disciples with the news: "I have seen the Lord!" And she told them that he had said these things to her. (Jn 20:17-18)

Without fear and without stipulations, Jesus sends Mary to make the most important announcement of the New Testament. Scholar James D. G. Dunn notes that an account like this was indeed radical in nature.

> Mary has the honour of reporting the empty tomb to the other disciples. . . . Yet, as is well known, in Middle Eastern

society of the time women were not regarded as reliable witnesses: a woman's testimony in court was heavily discounted. And any report that Mary had formerly been demon-possessed (Luke 8.2) would hardly add credibility to any story attributed to her in particular.[2]

Had this been a fabricated story, the writers would have never used a woman's account. In those days, women were rarely allowed to testify. Therefore, this story stood the test of potential ridicule and incredibility. But the story was told *as it happened*, and it wasn't because Mary was the only one at the tomb; it wasn't because there were no men, so Jesus had to send Mary; rather, this was an intentional, subversive, and radical move to send Mary. Time and again, Jesus boldly affirmed the value and worth of women, and appointed them to be colaborers in the mission. Jesus unabashedly elevated the traditional role of women so they too could participate in the work of the kingdom of God.[3] Women of the Bible were indeed *emboldened*.

Mary is not alone. With her is Phoebe, a deacon and a financial sponsor for Paul's missions; Priscilla, the gifted teacher; Mary, the mother of Jesus; and Junia, the bright and respected apostle who Scot McKnight calls a "Christ-experiencing, Christ-representing, church-establishing, probably miracle-working, missionizing woman who preached the gospel and taught the church."[4]

And then there are women such as Deborah, the fearless leader; Huldah, the prophet who helped reignite Israel's faith; Miriam, the gifted musician for the people of God; and Esther, the brave queen who seized the moment and boldly approached the king.

The very Spirit of the living God that caused a great earth-quake, shook the tomb, rolled the stone away, breathed *life* into Jesus' lungs, and raised Jesus from the dead, *emboldened* these women. And it is *this* Spirit, and *this* Jesus, who em-boldens women today.

THE YEAR WAS 340

It was an era typically attributed to the early church fathers, a time when theological disputes were constant and the condem-nation of heretics was at its peak. But this story isn't about one of the patristic fathers; instead, it's about a woman who fiercely taught God's truth in an era when women were almost totally silenced. After only seven months of marriage, Marcella became a widow and chose to live an ascetic religious life by devoting her life to God and the study of the Bible. She was well educated and a devoted learner. She was such an avid learner that she spent a lot of time at the feet of prominent scholar and Bible teacher Jerome, who is most well known for his Bible translation from Greek and Hebrew into Latin, and also for his mean-spirited nature toward women. But his posture toward women didn't intimidate Marcella; she refused to blindly accept any explanation of Jerome's and took him to task on many theological disputes. Highly esteemed by Jerome, Marcella was known for her biblical and theological brilliance, and for being on the front lines of condemning heretics. Jerome ennobles Marcella:

> And because my name was then especially esteemed in the
> study of the Scriptures, she never came without asking

something about Scripture, nor did she immediately accept my explanation as satisfactory, but she proposed questions from the opposite viewpoint, not for the sake of being contentious, but so that, by asking, she might learn solutions for points she perceived could be raised in objection. What virtue I found in her, what cleverness, what holiness, what purity, I am afraid to say, lest I exceed what belief finds credible. I will say only this, that whatever in us was gathered by long study and by lengthy meditation was almost changed into nature; this she tasted, this she learned, this she possessed. Thus, after my departure, if an argument arose about some evidence from Scripture, the question was pursued with her as the judge.[5]

Marcella pushed against the cultural norms and publicly called out heretics. Maybe Jerome saw her to be a "thorn in his side" for her refusal to accept simple answers, but she was brilliant, she was fierce, and she was a teacher.

This is our story! We are fierce, intellectually astute women who are brilliantly made to not accept simple answers. We are wise teachers and colleagues of some of the world's most renowned and brightest scholars. We look to men as colaborers in this great work and aren't afraid to push them to think in new capacities. This, my dear sisters, is our story.

THE YEAR WAS 1515

At the age of twenty-one, a grieving young woman who was devastated to leave her family joined the Carmelite Convent of the Incarnation at Ávila in Castile.[6] Teresa of Ávila eventually came to terms with her role and her love for the church. Although many might think she was tucked away in a convent with influence over women alone, through her writings her impact and influence have crossed both gender and denominational boundaries. Although she addresses women in her convents, some believe her writings are geared toward many priests and laymen.[7] She was a woman in tune with the depths of God through her commitment to contemplation. Even today, I hear many pastors—men included—attribute their passion for contemplation to the works of Teresa. From the walls of a convent, Teresa's words summon men and women alike to sit at her feet. Many have been shaped and formed by the Holy Spirit through her words.

This is our story! Our words live on and gather men and women alike to be nourished by our gifts, our words, and our passions. We find our voices, even when we begin with reluctance and fear. We put our words to paper and use them to call the bride to deeper places and edify her for mission. This, my dear sisters, is our story.

THE YEAR WAS 1880

Today, pastors like Steven Furtick, Bill Hybels, and Matt Chandler are known for their ministries that draw crowds as large as twenty-five thousand. But in 1880, it was a woman that drew such crowds. In those days, a woman in the pulpit was rare (they weren't even allowed to vote), but Maria Woodworth-Etter didn't let that stop her. She was on a mission from God. Almost immediately following her conversion as a teenager,

Woodworth-Etter received a call to the ministry, but this confused her because she saw only obstacles. Her denomination "did not believe that women had any right to work for Jesus," she recalls. "Had I told them my impression they would have made sport of me. I had never heard of women working in public except as missionaries, so I could see no openings—except, as I thought, if I ever married."[8]

She did marry, but this wasn't her doorway to ministry. Instead, she began following the leading of the Holy Spirit, and at the age of thirty-five she started preaching locally. Her ministry grew and was in such high demand that she was asked to lead countless local churches! But instead she began traveling coast to coast with an evangelistic ministry. Her ministry was interdenominational; she drew in people from every walk of the Christian faith. In 1912 and 1913 her camp meetings began to explode; as many as twenty-five thousand gathered for her preaching. The services were likened to stories found in the New Testament: "Thousands attended the meetings. The miracles were as great as in the days of Christ and the apostles. The fear of God came on the people as they saw the sick carried in, dying on beds, and then rise up and shout praises to God and walk and run. They saw them leap and dance."[9] People came far and wide to hear her preaching even as she grew weak with age. Woodworth-Etter was also a church planter. Near the end of her ministry, she planted a church that is still thriving and growing today: Lakeview Church, Indianapolis. ✳

This is our story! Even in an era when women have little to no rights in the public square, we rise up and are emboldened by the Holy Spirit to preach and teach. Even when we might be riddled with doubts and fear because we've never seen it done before, we choose obedience to the Spirit first and foremost. Even at the age of thirty-five, with no ministry training or education, and without a female role model, we *go for it*, because we can't imagine any other way. This, my dear sisters, is our story.

THE YEAR WAS 1977

Up until the 1970s, the debate about women in ministry in evangelical churches was mostly off the radar. For many women the 1970s were a ground-shaking, movement-making era. One of the movers and shakers of this time was Patricia Gundry, a passionate advocate for marginalized women in the church. Gundry wasn't okay with the status quo of women in the church and began to question some of those confusing passages in the Bible. To her surprise, she found out that hardly anyone was discussing some of those passages. Gundry described this in a 2006 interview:

> While serving a meal to a visiting preacher I asked him how he interpreted the passage [regarding women in the church] in 1 Timothy. To my shock and surprise, this man, who was usually very friendly and gracious, snapped at me, "Why do you want to know?!" He was sitting at my table, eating my spaghetti, and being obviously rude to me about a simple conversational question.
>
> That's when the light bulb moment came to me. I thought, He doesn't know. None of them know. But, they are willing to limit all women's lives and participation on the basis of Bible passages they know are problematic and

they don't know how to interpret. I determined to someday search and find the answers to my questions, and to share them with all other women who wanted to know too.[10]

After casually searching for answers, Gundry decided to take her research more seriously and authored *Woman Be Free!* (1977). ✷ Gundry was courageous, bold, and biblical in her writing, and she called on the church to no longer treat women as second-class citizens. In her ground-breaking book for its time, she tackled head-on many of the controversial passages for women in the church. Her book, however, was not without drama:

> Her conclusions appeared in 1977 as the book *Woman Be Free!* At the time of its release, Gundry's husband Stanley taught at the Moody Bible Institute, a conservative evangelical school in Chicago. According to Pat, people at Moody initially tried to ignore her book. Two years later, however, all that changed when she gave a lecture on women's rights in Glen Ellyn, a suburb geographically close to Moody. Conservative Christians sent scores of letters to Moody objecting that the wife of a Moody professor was speaking out for women's rights. Eventually Moody banned Pat Gundry from its media and on August 1, 1979, asked Stan Gundry to resign, since he and his wife were an embarrassment to the school.[11]

Although it took time, attention was drawn to Gundry's work, which eventually led to the founding of Christians for Biblical Equality, an important ministry still in existence today. Gundry's was a voice in the wilderness crying out for equality for women in the church. She pushed against the norms and refused to accept the sidelining of women in the church.

This is our story! We are voices in the wilderness; we are prophetic. We are bold enough to say the things that no one else is saying, and we are willing to speak up for the marginalized. We are Bible teachers, and Bible expositors; we cry out for justice, and we do it with class, love, and grace. This, my dear sisters, is our story.

THIS IS MY STORY TOO!

I was a seemingly typical 1990s teenager living sixty miles south of Chicago on a forty-acre horse farm. Stacks of boy band CDs garnished my nightstand—NSYNC, Boyz II Men, Backstreet Boys, and 98 Degrees to name a few. "I Wanna Love You Forever" by Jessica Simpson was my jam; I would often stand on my bed and sing it at the top of my lungs, with a hairbrush as my microphone, imagining I was singing it to my latest high school crush. Rarely did I ever leave my house without my Clinique Almost Lipstick in Black Honey or my CK Perfume. I was so boy crazy and usually had a date to homecoming, winter ball, or prom. I would spend months picking out a dress, and an entire day getting ready for makeup and hair.

I was typical, but something changed around sixteen. I was alone in my bedroom and had just finished reading the entire Gospel of Luke in one sitting. When I got to the story of the cross, I was overcome with gratitude—pure, unhindered gratitude. I didn't know what else to do, so I got down on my knees next to my bed, lifted my hands in the air, and began to whisper, "Thank you, Jesus. Thank you, Jesus. Thank you, Jesus." Eventually, my whisper turned into passionate shouts with giant tears of joy streaming down my face and onto my bed. For the next hour and a half the only words that came out of my mouth were, "Thank you, Jesus. Thank you, Jesus." My prayer was simple—it wasn't formulated, it wasn't fancy, and it certainly wasn't poetic. But it was real, and it was raw.

After that day in the bedroom, a holy stirring took over my drowsy soul. There was an awakening, an explosion of sorts—a Holy Spirit emboldening. Completely on fire, I was now a teenager on mission. I had to tell my parents, my brothers, and my friends—heck, I had to tell the entire high school, and I practically did. I was one of those teenagers. Every single Monday night, I would illegally pile a dozen or more kids into my Toyota RAV4 and take them all to the local Youth for Christ gathering. One by one my friends were coming to Christ. We were all experiencing calls into ministry, including me. We all wanted to see our high school transformed for the glory of Jesus. So we started gathering around our high school flagpole every single night to pray. We prayed for the Holy Spirit to move in our high school; we prayed for our friends to experience the life-changing power of Jesus Christ; we prayed for the brokenhearted to find healing.

We were desperate to see this thing we read about in church history called revival. We prayed for revival. We prayed for movement. We prayed for life change, and we saw all of it.

Every day when I got home from school, I would quickly eat my dinner, finish my homework, and then sprint to my bedroom. As soon as my door was closed, I would blast worship music on my stereo and pace my room in prayer. I was sixteen.

I am certain that my prayers would have made most theologians squirm. (I squirm myself today when I think about them. But they were me, and they were real, and they were filled with God's Spirit.) My prayers wouldn't have moved a congregation to repentance. My prayers weren't fancy, but they were raw. I wanted to see more of Jesus. They were full of passion, full of life. After praying, I would grab my Bible and read, journal, and pray the Scriptures. My prayer journal was so honest, so unhindered, so adoring of God.

A couple of years later, my girlfriends and I piled into my car, drove down some country roads blasting "My Redeemer Lives" by Nicole C. Mullen, and eventually pulled over to some cornfield. Together, we belted out "I know, my Redeemer lives!" to the stars as the fireflies danced in the humid Midwestern cornfield. About halfway through the song, I pulled out my Bible, turned toward the cornfield, and began to preach. And I mean preach. I don't remember who exactly I was preaching to other than my girlfriends and stalks of corn, and I don't remember what I was preaching about, but I do remember thinking that I knew preaching was going to be my trajectory. I must have imagined the cornstalks were thousands of people, and the Spirit was stirring something inside of me that night.

In those days, it rarely dawned on me that I would experience resistance because I was a woman. It didn't dawn on me that I would someday be snubbed or ignored. Occasionally, when I was a teenager, I heard things like "women can't be senior pastors" or "God only calls women to be senior pastors when men don't step up." Or I'd hear, "You're such a godly young woman, you're going to make a man very happy someday as a wife and mother." Usually, when I heard these things, I ignored them because I was so certain that God was calling me to preach.

I have faced enough resistance to send me to my knees and drench my pillow with tears. But I am still an emboldened woman in ministry. I am emboldened because of the great calling God has placed on my life, and I am emboldened because of all of the men and women who have opened up doors for me, spoken words of wisdom, and affirmed my gifts.

FOR ME THE YEAR WAS 2008

"Your voice is important and needed in our context," said Pastor Glen, teaching pastor at Good Shepherd Church in Naperville, Illinois. "We need you preaching in the pulpit," he encouraged. I wanted to believe him, I really did, but something inside of me at first fought back.

I was a few years out of college and a spring chicken in ministry. Upon graduation with a BA in ministry, I had dreams of standing behind the pulpit, preaching the Word of God, much like I had seen many men do in my church tradition.

I was fortunate to have many wonderful, affirming opportunities in my youth pastor role in the lovely rural church in upstate New York. I had many preaching bloopers at that church, but the congregation loved me anyway, and the senior pastor always went out of his way to affirm my gifts and calling. Rarely did a day go by that he wouldn't offer words of encouragement.

But when my husband and I moved back to the Chicago area, I was eager to land a pastoral position in a local church. I excitedly began writing emails, making phone calls, and doing everything possible to contact leaders in our denomination's district. After months of assertive communications, I heard nothing. Not even a response from the district denominational leader. No one reached out to me. I began feeling as if I didn't matter, or worse—as if I didn't even exist. *Maybe you're not really called. Maybe you heard God wrong. Maybe you aren't gifted. Maybe you should pursue something else.* These words, in my voice, rattled around in my head. When I imagined myself standing in the pulpit, I at times saw myself as an imposter.

I began to pursue a career in what I knew how to do well, riding and training horses. I grew up on a small horse farm and was a competitive rider. I thought, if the church doesn't want me, I'll share the good news of Jesus in the horse industry. I began riding north of six horses a day and giving lessons to young students. But every night when I would get in my car to make my way home, dirt in my teeth, exhausted from the hot sun, I wasn't dreaming about jumping six-foot oxers on my dream horse. I wasn't dreaming about winning my first Grand Prix or making my first $100,000 on a horse sale. Instead, I had visions of studying the Bible in research for hours on end and then teaching the all-consuming, all-powerful, all-encouraging truth to the body of Christ. I ached for it. I longed for it. And at the end of every evening, I would pull away from the barn and these dreams, these visions, these hopes would carry my thoughts away until I pulled up into my driveway. I knew that I could no longer run.

Eventually, my yearning found me sitting behind a computer screen, sending my résumé out to a few churches. The résumés led to interviews and then a job offer for a part-time senior high youth director position at a church of four thousand in Naperville.

I eagerly accepted the call and jumped in with both feet. After a month of serving at Good Shepherd Church, one of the teaching pastors pulled me into his office and affirmed the gifts he saw in me. Pastor Glen said, "Your voice is important and needed in our context. How do you feel about preaching on a Sunday morning two weeks from now?" Preaching? Me? I had such a hard time believing that they would actually allow me to stand behind their pulpit. "Of course, yes! Yes!"

I was twenty-six years old, barely believing in myself. I preached a sermon to a loving, kind, and affirming group. The rest of the pastors heard me preach and kept inviting me back to the pulpit, eventually inviting me to the teaching team where I got to preach one to two times a month. Weeks turned into months, and months turned into years, and I had the joy of serving on the teaching team for over five years.

The pastors were my champions. Many times my insecurities would creep in, and I would question whether I was equipped to preach a particular sermon, but the pastors would practically shove me to the pulpit. Why? They believed in me, and I knew it. They didn't just tell me, they showed me. They mentored me, they championed my call, they sent me to seminary, and most significantly they gave me countless opportunities to exercise my gifts.

Like a weak baby tree budding in a nurturing tree nursery, I took root and grew at and with Good Shepherd Church. And I blossomed because of pastors believing in me, mentoring me, and giving me incredible opportunities.

I am emboldened first and foremost because of the resurrecting and transforming power of the Spirit who calls me and

empowers me to use my gifts for the church; I am emboldened
when I read about the women of the Bible; I am emboldened
by a family who believes in me; and I am emboldened by
countless pastors, laypeople, friends, professors, and family.

THE YEAR IS NOW

Today I am an emboldened woman. Every week I serve, love,
pastor, nurture, lead, and preach to a congregation I love so
very deeply. First Church of the Nazarene of Pasadena
(PazNaz) is a historic, intergenerational, intercultural, and
missional church of roughly nineteen hundred members just
outside of Los Angeles. Together we love Jesus and join Jesus
on mission in our local and global neighborhoods. My role as
the senior pastor of this church is not just a job or a career
aspiration, but an outflow of a deep, abiding love for King
Jesus, the bride, and the mission of God. As an emboldened
woman, there was once a time I never would have dreamed
that I would be doing what I *get to do*. Most weeks I pinch
myself as I am walking into my office and whisper to myself,
"Is this real life?" It is real life, and I am an emboldened woman
at an emboldened church, thanks to many who helped get me
here. Many factors could have kept me from this moment, but
there's always been a fire in my bones to never stop preaching,
teaching, leading, and evangelizing. "Nothing . . . is impossible with God" (Lk 1:37 *The Message*). And for that I am an
emboldened woman.

Emboldened women stand on the sweat and tears of risk
takers who have gone before us. They have paved the way and
opened doors that would have been too heavy for any one

person to open. Every Sunday morning when I stand in the pulpit to preach and teach, I stand there because I have been emboldened by women who have boldly gone before me.

This is our story, and it is permeated with good news for women in ministry. Ours is a story to celebrate, to proclaim from the rooftops; we continue this legacy with much pride and honor. These days, we all too often focus *only* on the negative experiences for women in ministry. But we mustn't forget that there is also much to celebrate. We have a story to tell and to live into. My dear sisters, may we boldly and fiercely step into the future as emboldened women like Mary, or as a warrior like Deborah, or as a brilliant thinker like Marcella, or as a passionate preacher like Maria Woodworth-Etter. Now is our time to rise up and live into what God has created us to do: serve the bride of Christ and participate in the mission of God.

TWO

OVERCOMING IMPOSTER SYNDROME

EVERY CHRISTMAS, one of my family's favorite traditions is to watch the movie *Elf*.[1] One of the scenes that usually has us rolling on the floor in laughter is when Buddy the elf meets "Santa" in the department store. The scene goes something like this:

BUDDY	Santa!

Santa enters. Children and Buddy cheer and call out.

BUDDY	Who the heck are you?
SANTA	What are you talking about? I'm Santa Claus.
BUDDY	No you're not!
SANTA	Why of course I am! Ho! Ho! Ho!
BUDDY	If you're Santa, what song did I sing for you on your birthday this year?
SANTA	Uh . . . Happy Birthday, of course.
SANTA	*(To little boy on lap)* So how old are you son? You're a big boy. What's your name?
LITTLE BOY	Paul.

SANTA	What do you want for Christmas?
BUDDY	Paul, don't tell him what you want. He's a liar. *(to Santa)* You disgust me! How can you live with yourself?
SANTA	Just cool it, Zippy!
BUDDY	You sit on a throne of *lies*.
SANTA	*(getting angry)* Look, I'm not kidding . . .
BUDDY	You're a fake!
SANTA	I'm a fake? How'd you like to be dead?
LITTLE BOY	*(whispering)* Fake.
SANTA	*(to the little boy, laughing)* He's kidding!
BUDDY	You stink! You smell like beef and cheese. You don't smell like Santa.

Buddy pulls off Santa's beard.

BUDDY	He's an *imposter*! *(Santa tackles Buddy . . . they begin wrestling)* He's a fake! He's a fake! He's not Santa Claus!

(A fight ensues. "Santa" chases Buddy around the store while kids scream in horror.)

This might possibly be the funniest scene in the entire movie. Santa was indeed an imposter and was found out by Buddy the elf. Strangely, I can relate to the imposter in this scene, and maybe you can too.

When I stepped into my first year at Northern Seminary in 2011, I had a nine-month-old at home, and I was serving in full-time ministry at a large church in the western suburbs of Chicago. Although I had been given many opportunities to teach and preach, and although I had good grades in college in both Bible and theology, and although I was doing well in seminary, and though I knew God not only called me but also gifted me, I was still convinced I was a total fraud and didn't really belong in the pulpit, let alone higher education.

After my first year at Northern Seminary, my favorite New Testament scholar and author, Scot McKnight, joined the faculty. I had read several of his books and was a regular reader of his blog, and now he was going to teach at Northern Seminary. I'll never forget the first paper I submitted to him. As soon as I hit the "send" button, I had an overwhelming feeling that everything was about to come crashing down. A couple of days later when Dr. McKnight returned my paper, I was terrified to open it. I took a deep breath and clicked on the email with racing heart and sweating palms. To my total shock, he gave me an A and even said "well done." I sat at my computer screen and stared at the grade and at the feedback. But these were my thoughts: *He only gave me an A because I was engaged in class and interested in the subject. He didn't really like my paper; he just didn't want to hurt my feelings.*

Paper after paper I received As and paper after paper I was always in utter disbelief. I rarely spoke up in class like my male classmates because something stupid was bound to come out of my mouth (so I thought).

Whether it's preaching a sermon, leading a board, writing a paper, or using our gifts in any capacity, feeling like an imposter is not uncommon for women. It turns out there is an actual name for this: *imposter syndrome.* In her book *Lean In,* Sheryl Sandberg describes it like this:

For women, feeling like a fraud is a symptom of a greater problem. We consistently underestimate ourselves. Multiple studies in multiple industries show that women often judge their own performance as worse than it actually is, while men judge their own performance as better than it actually is. Assessments of students in a surgery rotation found that when asked to evaluate themselves, the female students gave themselves lower scores than the male students despite the faculty evaluations that showed the women outperformed the men. A survey of several thousand potential political candidates revealed that despite having comparable credentials, the men were about 60 percent more likely to think that they were "very qualified" to run for political office. A study of close to one thousand Harvard law students found that in almost every category of skills relevant to practicing law, women gave themselves lower scores than men. Even worse, when women evaluate themselves in front of other people or in stereotypically male domains, their underestimations can become even more pronounced.[2]

No doubt about it, this is a common problem for women and minorities. As a result, many women feel as though they are simply faking it. This, I believe, absolutely translates to women in ministry. Women who are capable and compelling teachers and preachers, women who are brilliant theologians and scholars, and women who are magnetic leaders are simply unable to embrace their God-given giftedness. Although a woman has clear ability and giftedness, and although others recognize her giftedness and ability, there is an *inability* on the part of the woman to internalize that giftedness as genuine. When a woman is called, gifted, and recognized as gifted but is unable to embrace her giftedness, we see the imposter syndrome. It is not whether a woman *has a gift* but whether she can *internalize* this as true. This, in part, is due to a landscape in which males have created a culture of leadership fit for males and seemingly unfit for women.

When I was navigating a call process for a lead pastor role, my husband and I went out to dinner with some very good friends. Over dinner, we were discussing the opportunity. When I explained the job potential and began to reflect on my own abilities out loud, I explained to them how unqualified I was for the role. In fact, I went on and on and on for twenty minutes on how hilarious it was that this church was actually interested in such an unqualified individual. Our friends politely listened to me rattle on, but then at the end of the evening my friend Amy reminded me of a stunning reality. "You know, Tara Beth, I could never imagine a man saying the things that you have said tonight." And it hit me; she was right. My old friend imposter syndrome had the wheel of my discernment process for this call. Sheryl Sandberg says it right:

> Ask a man to explain his success and he will typically credit his own innate qualities and skills. Ask a woman the same question and she will attribute her success to external factors, insisting she did well because she "worked really hard" or "got lucky," or "had help from others." Men and women also differ when it comes to explaining failure.[3]

At the beginning of the call process, I was convinced that the church was interested in me for anything *but my gifts and skills*. I couldn't see that maybe they were interested in me for my twelve years of ministry in megachurches. I had a hard time admitting that I had skills, experience, and gifting to lead, shepherd, and pastor a church. I was blind to the idea that maybe they *were actually interested in me for me*—Tara Beth—a supernaturally gifted leader, teacher, preacher, and pastor, totally emboldened by the Spirit.

While there are many factors and systems that keep women sidelined in the church, imposter syndrome is one of them. I think of my friend Madison who grew up in a loving, Spirit-filled church. As a little girl, her parents read Scriptures to her, discipled her, and made sure she went to church Sunday after Sunday. And Sunday after Sunday as she sat in the pews, she saw male preachers, male worship leaders, male ushers, male elders, male denominational leaders, and male evangelists. She saw plenty of women serving in the church, but they were usually secretaries or in the kitchen organizing meals or ministering through the prayer-shawl ministry or attending women's Bible studies.

When Madison was in high school, she witnessed her male youth pastor spend more time with the guys in her youth group and give them opportunities to even teach, lead, and preach. When Madison got to college, she joined a campus ministry led by men. One day someone came alongside of Madison and began to affirm gifts that they had seen in her. This friend told Madison that she was a gifted communicator, she knew the Bible, and she was always leading friends to

Christ. This friend encouraged Madison to pray about whether her gifts could be used in full-time ministry for the body of Christ. But Madison laughed. *That would be impossible*, she thought. When she closed her eyes and imagined herself leading, teaching, and evangelizing, she saw an imposter. Of course she did, she had no idea how to imagine a woman leading in such a way.

Madisons are in every church, every youth group, and every campus ministry. Madisons sit in our pews and wonder what their narrative is within the body of Christ, and they have a hard time seeing that the gifts they bring to the table have anything to do with participating in the great mission of God in this world. Instead, because of what they have always seen, and because of what they have always known, they see that task as for their brothers in Christ. Therefore, when Madison is called into ministry, imposter syndrome is only a symptom of the male-shaped culture that is happening within the body of Christ.

IS THAT YOU, GOD?

Knowing that imposter syndrome is a side effect that many women in ministry might have to endure for at least the near future, how can we help women in ministry navigate this challenge? First, awareness is key. When doubt, fear of failure, or insecurity creeps in, we can ask ourselves, does this sound like God? Let's take a look at Scripture and discover together how God sees us.

Imagine the scene for a moment. Jesus is having a conversation with his disciples, and one of the disciples, Philip, says, "Lord, show us the Father and that will be enough for us." Jesus, probably a little flustered with Philip, says "Don't you know me, Philip, even after I have been among you such a long time? Anyone who has seen me has seen the Father" (Jn 14:8-9). And then Jesus, after explaining to Philip the unity between himself and the Father, says,

> Very truly I tell you, whoever believes in me will do the works I have been doing, and they will do even greater things than these, because I am going to the Father. And I will do whatever you ask in my name, so that the Father may be glorified in the Son. You may ask me for anything in my name, and I will do it. (Jn 14:12-14)

Such a profound and even overwhelming promise from the mouth of Jesus! What could Jesus possibly have meant by this? First, notice *who* Jesus says will do "greater things": believers. Will those who believe in Jesus actually be able to participate in the work of Jesus and even do greater things? Why yes, yes we can. Notice the qualifications aren't based on gender, not *even on pastoral title*, but on *believing—no exclusions*. In other words, those who put their trust in Jesus as Lord and lean into the empowering presence of the Spirit can participate *in the same mission Jesus participated in: redeeming the world to himself*. Jesus did this through (1) miraculous signs such as healing, (2) preaching, (3) teaching, (4) prophesying, (5) evangelizing, (6) caring for the sick, (7) radical acts of love, and (8) laying down his life.

Jesus says, whoever *believes* in me will also do the works that I do. We, then, as sons and *daughters* of the King will participate in the mission of God in this world through miracles, teaching, preaching, prophesying, evangelizing, caring for the sick, radical acts of love, and laying down our lives for others. By believing in Jesus, by being so united with him through the Spirit, we will bear witness to the world about Jesus—the world will see Jesus *in us* through our work. This is all awesome and astonishing on so many levels, but here's what I want you to get: Just as we believe in Jesus, *so Jesus believes in us.* Dear sister, Jesus believes in *you.* Maybe it's time to pause for a moment, take a deep breath, and allow those words to soak into your heart. Jesus believes in you; you are not an imposter.

Before there was Michael Phelps, there was Tom Jager— "the bullet." In his day, Tom was the fastest swimmer in the world and held the record for the fifty meter freestyle. When I was fifteen years old I was accepted into the Gold Medal Swim Camp near Albuquerque, New Mexico, with Tom Jager himself. This swim camp was only for the emerging fastest swimmers; I wasn't one of them. I was accepted into the camp because of my brother, a swimmer on the Olympic training swim team.[4]

Swim practice after swim practice, set after set, I was always the last to finish; I was the slowest. To say that I felt like an imposter at that swim camp would be a total understatement. When the day came to hike a local mountain with all one hundred campers, I was, of course, the last in line. Dead last. The altitude and intensity of the climb was more than my lungs could handle, and I found myself hyperventilating every ten minutes. Consequently, I was holding up the rest of the campers. Near the end of the climb, thinking I was about at the end of my rope, I collapsed on a rock with nothing left to give. Ready to throw in the towel, I looked up to a line of about one hundred frustrated campers and saw 6'3" Tom Jager making his way down from the mountain to the end of the line. With his hand held out, he said, "Come on, Tara Beth, we will do this together; *I believe in you.*"

Dear sister, maybe you feel like I did on the mountain that day. Maybe you feel like you've joined a swim camp that you never should have been to in the first place. Maybe you feel like you don't belong, like you're an imposter. Hear these words: Jesus believes in you, Jesus is with you, and Jesus will equip you. And may we, his daughters, begin to *believe* that he *believes in us.*

RELEASING THE CHAINS OF IMPOSTER SYNDROME

The Spirit of the living God emboldens and empowers us to be released from the chains of imposter syndrome. Imagine the day of Pentecost, when the empowering presence of the Holy Spirit fell upon *all* of God's people. Peter—filled with this Spirit—boldly stood before the masses and declared:

In the last days, God says,
    I will pour out my Spirit on all people.

Your sons and daughters will prophesy,
    your young men will see visions,
    your old men will dream dreams.

Even on my servants, both men and women,
    I will pour out my Spirit in those days,
    and they will prophesy. (Acts 2:17-18, emphasis added)

This same Holy Spirit inspires men and women alike; there are no distinctions in God's new kingdom. The people of God are living into the eschatological vision proclaimed by the apostle Peter. Empowered by the Spirit, women are living the life of the future *here and now* just by using their gifts to edify the church (1 Cor 12:4-11; Rom 12:4-8; Eph 4:11-13). Therefore, when women are included in this mission, the people of God get a glimpse of this eschatological vision as proclaimed by Jesus and the apostle Peter, and the chains of imposter syndrome are released as together we are propelled into God's glorious mission.[5]

Women in the church are consistently underestimating themselves and the gifts God has given them, but when we look to the emboldening presence of the Holy Spirit, our perspective begins to change. Let's take a look at Acts 4, for example. The early church was fresh off its honeymoon, and opposition was now on the rise. While John and Peter were preaching and teaching, they were seized and thrown into jail. The following day, Peter and John stood before the opponents. Hear what follows:

> They had Peter and John brought before them and began to question them: "By what power or what name did you do this?"
>
> Then Peter, filled with the Holy Spirit, said to them: "Rulers and elders of the people! If we are being called to account today for an act of kindness shown to a man who was lame and are being asked how he was healed, then know this, you and all the people of Israel: It is by the

name of Jesus Christ of Nazareth, whom you crucified but whom God raised from the dead, that this man stands before you healed. Jesus is

　　"'the stone you builders rejected,

　　which has become the cornerstone.'

Salvation is found in no one else, for there is no other name under heaven given to mankind by which we must be saved."

When they saw the courage of Peter and John and realized that they were unschooled, ordinary men, they were astonished and they took note that these men had been with Jesus. (Acts 4:7-13)

Peter and John, filled with the Spirit, were given courage to stand and proclaim the gospel in the face of opposition. After being released, Peter and John returned to their people and continued to preach in the power of the Spirit, and prayed for the people of God. Notice what they prayed: "Now, Lord, consider their threats and enable your servants to speak your word with great boldness" (Acts 4:29). Peter, filled with the Holy Spirit, had noticeable *courage* in the face of opposition. Not only that, but the disciples passionately believed in the *emboldening* power of the Spirit, so they prayed that other believers would speak the word with *boldness*.

Similarly, the apostle Paul, chained in prison, experiencing the epitome of opposition, writes to the Ephesians and makes this request, "Pray also for me, that whenever I speak, words may be given me so that I will *fearlessly* make known the mystery of the gospel" (Eph 6:19, emphasis added).

Peter and John, and then also Paul, understood better than almost anyone the hardships that ministry brings. But hardship didn't stop them; rather, they looked to the emboldening presence of the Spirit to give them courage to proclaim the gospel in order to make Christ known, which leads us to an important point. The apostles in the early church weren't given boldness and courage just so they could *withstand opposition*, but they were given boldness and courage because they were *ambassadors of the gospel*. In the same way, *women in the church* are ambassadors of the gospel and have been given this same Spirit to use their gifts with *boldness* so the mission of God will continue to advance in this world. It is the *same Spirit* who empowered the ministry of Jesus; the *same Spirit* who raised Jesus from the dead; the *same Spirit* who launched the early church into the world's grandest movement, and it is the *same Spirit* who brings victory over the powers that chain women in the church, including imposter syndrome.

The life, fulfillment, death, resurrection, and ascension of King Jesus, and the empowering of the Holy Spirit, offer a new reality—this changes everything. The imposter point of view, if we let it, can keep women sidelined within the body of Christ, but as daughters of the resurrection, we claim the resurrection life *here and now*. As daughters of the resurrection, then, we choose power, boldness, and courage. As one of the greatest scholars on the Holy Spirit, Gordon Fee, says, "The Spirit means the presence of great power, power to overflow with hope (Romans 15:3), power sometimes attested by signs and wonders."[6] May women, then, be a sign and wonder of the work of the Spirit in our world.

OWN YOUR OWN UNIQUE VOICE

When I began my journey in ministry in the very early 2000s, I accepted a role as senior high youth pastor in a church in upstate New York. While I was delighted to begin using my teaching, preaching, and pastoral gifts, I was still navigating what I thought a youth pastor was supposed to look, sound, and act like. Up until then, I had never known a female youth pastor. I was discipled in a wonderful parachurch ministry, Youth for Christ, where all of the directors were male, and my youth pastor and pastor in my local congregation were male. I had *never* heard a woman preach, but I still *knew* it was my calling, and I was still confused by what it looked like for a woman to teach, preach, and lead. Shortly after beginning my ministry at the church, they graciously sent my husband and me away to attend a mega-youth ministry conference.

While we were there, I couldn't even tell you how many times my husband was approached and asked where *he* serves as a youth pastor, while I was standing right next to him. And while the conference was an edifying experience for me, it was also discouraging. I had encountered a strange subculture. Maybe you've seen this subculture of youth pastors— it's a phenomenon, really. When I walked through this mega-conference of some six thousand youth pastors, I realized that 99 percent of them were male with some sort of statement facial hair. (In the late 90s, it was a goatee with wide-legged pants; in the early 2000s, it was a soul patch with dark-rimmed glasses and skinny jeans. Today, it's likely a lumberjack beard with rolled-up jeans.) And every speaker that graced the main stage seemed to fit into this subculture and was also hilarious, told a lot of sports jokes, and had a certain style of communicating.

Session after session I began to feel more and more like an outsider. But, like most youth pastors, I was a learner and wanted to take what I had learned to my students in upstate New York. Instead of simply taking some great information about youth ministry, I also took with me the assumed image of youth pastors. I tried to be funny, and that never worked; I tried to be sporty, and that was awkward; I tried to be loud and outgoing, and that was exhausting; I tried to be trendy, and that was uncomfortable. The more stops I pulled, the more masks I wore, the more I tried to be somebody I was not, the more I dreaded ministry. Bless the church in New York, they saw a shifting Tara Beth and loved me anyway!

The point is this: when a ministerial culture is created by men, women are often unsure of their footing and therefore unsure of how they are to look and act. It's no wonder so many women feel like total frauds! But whoever you are—male or female, minority or privileged—hear this: God has given *you* a voice that is *your voice*. God has gifted you in ways that are unique to you. Hear the wise words of pastor Mandy Smith:

> When we as leaders have an important message or a huge task, we pull out all the stops—lights, music, production. But over and over, when God has some serious business to take care of, he goes small and obscure. . . . Whether or not we talk about it, we're aware of our own limitation. This is especially true when we're faced with the challenges of ministry. We're reminded every day how we're

not witty or educated or talented enough. And when we get that sinking feeling of knowing our own limitations, when we're dragged down by the weight of our own emptiness, we want to do whatever we can to fix it. We desperately work harder, hoping that if we're perfect this time it will be okay. We wear ourselves out, trying to match a preconceived ideal. . . . And the more desperate we feel, the more we try to mask how far in over our heads we are, hoping no one will be able to tell.[7]

When women see those who serve in ministry, we quickly realize we look different from the rest. Furthermore, not all women fit into a single mold! I grew up with a mom who stayed home with her kids from the time we were little until high school. She loved to bake, garden, craft, and carefully decorate the house. Jackie Roese describes it with creativity in her book *Lime Green*. She describes types of women through colors:

> Coming to Dallas as a brand new Christian who had never been around other Christians nor really attended any church, I quickly learned Christian women are supposed to be light pink. That's the color I saw when I went to my first Women's Bible study in North Dallas at Northwest Bible Church. I'm known for saying, "Texas women know how to be women!" That's what I saw. Women, dressed to the nines with shoes, bags, and jewelry to match. Their makeup tastefully done. Their fingernails well manicured. Many of the older women had nicer figures than my twenty-something shape. (I later learned you can buy that better shape.)

The women seemed quieter, nicer—True Blue Southern Belles. I, on the other hand, just got off the boat, so to speak, from New York. Sarcasm, directness, and swearing were normative for northeasterners. . . .

My hair was unruly. I never learned how to manage my wild mane. . . . I didn't wear makeup, I never had a manicure, nor did I own a fancy purse. I found backpacks to be way more functional. I felt like I was in a foreign country. . . .

Over time I found myself thinking, *If I'm going to be a good Christian woman, then I need to be more like them. I need to get some makeup, a red purse, and I need to be nicer and quieter!*[8]

Later, Jackie learned that she wasn't *light pink* but perhaps lime green. In the body of Christ, we have orange, yellow, magenta, red, sage, and every color of the spectrum. As Jackie beautifully illustrates, all colors are equally called to participate in the mission of God.

The most tempting route might be to pull out all the stops and not be *who* we're called to be. It took me years to figure out that I didn't have to be somebody else; I only had to be who God created and gifted me to be. I preach in a certain way only because of how I was formed in a very specific context, a very specific family, and a very specific culture. Many years later I realized that although I am not a funny storyteller or a jokester, I am an emotive preacher; and although I don't engage people through sports, I do engage them as a nurturing pastor; and although I am not an authoritative leader, I am a relational leader. I am who I am, and I have been gifted as I am, and I'm not sorry for it.

Sisters in Christ, it is my hope that you lead, teach, preach, shepherd, evangelize, and equip in the way that only you—in the Spirit—can do. *And do it with confidence; do it with gusto.*[9] ✳

THREE

BREAKING STEREOTYPES

I STOOD IN OUR YARD and leaned over our fence to talk with another parent on the other side. Both of my boys were playing peekaboo with her little boy. I had never met this neighbor, and we were delighted to discover that our boys might have a neighborhood playmate. We sipped our morning coffees as we chatted about toddler development, preschools, our husbands' jobs, and neighborhood life. Eventually, she asked whether I stayed home with the boys or if I was a working mom. Her response was one of shock; not because I work but because I am a pastor. "A pastor? You don't look like one! Can women even be pastors?" I'm not sure if it was because I had a messy bun on top of my head or if it was the yoga pants, but her imagination just couldn't place me in ministry. This, however, is a conversation I often have, and a response I often hear.[1]

It's tempting, then, to try to squeeze myself into some sort of norm that I'll never fit. For example, somewhere deeply ingrained in my psyche is the notion that nurturing and maternal traits are not leadership traits. Maybe it's ingrained in yours too. In fact, there have been plenty who have said that the "feminization of the church" will be the demise of the church—as if feminine traits are negative, weak, and cause for decline. Naturally, then, when I lead with what is sometimes linked to feminine traits, it's a temptation for me to feel doubtful, or worse, shameful. And sometimes I exemplify a web of traits that are a source of shame. For example, if I show emotion, will I risk looking emotionally unstable? If I am ambitious, will I risk looking dangerously aggressive? If I wear a fashionable outfit while preaching, will I risk the perception of being a seductress? If I am a relational and collaborative leader, will I risk not being decisive enough? If I'm assertive, will I risk being called too masculine or even angry? If I choose to pastor full-time and not stay home with my kids, will I risk being perceived as a bad mom?

Managing our own perceptions and worrying about others can be exhausting. But God has been growing me, and giving me peace with who I am as a leader, teacher, preacher, and pastor. God has gifted me in ways that are unique to me. God has given me a perspective as a mother and a nurturer, which will spill out plenty of times. And just because I've never seen that from a pastor doesn't mean it's *wrong*. While a nurturing mother is the furthest thing from our minds when we think of *leader*, Scripture is full of rich imagery describing God with maternal and nurturing traits. For example:

> It was I who taught Ephraim to walk,
>   taking them by the arms;
> but they did not realize
>   it was I who healed them.
> I led them with cords of human kindness,
>   with ties of love.

To them I was like one who lifts
a little child to the cheek.
I bent down to feed them. (Hos 11:3-4)

Like an eagle that stirs up its nest,
and hovers over its young,
that spreads its wings to catch them
and carries them aloft. (Deut 32:11)

As a mother comforts her child,
so I will comfort you;
and you will be comforted over Jerusalem. (Is 66:13)

Even the apostle Paul saw himself with nurturing and maternal traits:

We were like young children among you.

Just as a nursing mother cares for her children, so we cared for you. Because we loved you so much, we were delighted to share with you not only the gospel of God but our lives as well. (1 Thess 2:7-8)

While culture might paint maternal traits as something to be removed from leadership, Scripture flips this upside down and shows them as a *strength*. Maternal and nurturing leaders, like mothers, seek not only to care for but also push for the success of their families. They nurture in times that call for empathy, presence, and care, but they also push, inspire, and motivate.

A DEEP MATERNAL LOVE FOR PAZNAZ

I loved her. The more I studied her, the more I spent time with her, and the more I walked alongside her with a nurturing presence, I loved her even more. She was beautiful beyond words, and I was in awe that I got to be *her* pastor—the local church in Pasadena, that is.

On my fifteenth week as their new senior pastor, I closed out our series "Wired for Mission." We had been studying for thirteen straight weeks the first missional church in the book of Acts, and we had been discovering together what it meant that we, together, were created for mission. It was more than just a preaching series—it was my heart, longing, and dreams for the local church. So as I ended the series I called the congregation into a time of corporate prayer and response. At the end of the prayer, I invited people to stand with me as a declaration to me, to one another, and to God, that we would indeed be a local church *on mission* in Pasadena. After a time of prayer and worship, I stood up and faced the congregation to pray and deliver the benediction, and as I turned around I observed 100 percent of the congregation standing with me. They were *all in.* Many were proudly smiling, and many were weeping tears of joy. Although I had told them many times before this moment, I told them again, with tears streaming down my face and a lump in my throat: "First Church of the Nazarene of Pasadena, there is no other local church on this planet that I would rather pastor. I am honored to be on mission with you, and I am honored to call myself your pastor. *I love you more than I even know how to say.*"

The emotions of that moment felt similar to the emotions I first experienced on April 17, 2010, when my son, Caleb Daniel Leach, was placed into my arms for the first time. As I held Caleb, tears streamed down my face and onto his precious cheeks. All I could think about was how amazing it was that

God had allowed me to love such a precious child. I was madly in love. He was beautiful. I studied his fingers, his tiny toes, his gigantic eyelashes, and his chubby cheeks. The more I studied, the more in love I grew. As I held him I prayed with a lump in my throat, "Lord, I am in awe that you have made something so beautiful and have now entrusted me to walk with this child, love this child, nurture this child, and lead this child." Similarly, as I looked out to my beloved congregation in Pasadena, I was in awe that God had entrusted me to walk with them, love them, nurture them, and lead them.

I have always had a pastor's heart, and pastors are most certainly loving and present. But since the office of the senior pastor in the North American evangelical church is primarily held by men, I have never had the opportunity to watch a female senior pastor lead, and I have actually ever only known one (although I know two others that are copastors with their husbands). I have had the best mentors, influencers, teachers, and professors who have helped get me where I am today, but I have never seen a female *senior* pastor lead. Furthermore, whenever I meet someone new I usually hear something along the lines of "Wow, *you're the senior pastor*! You're beautiful!" I can't blame them for being shocked. I don't look the part. I look more like the young suburban mom who enjoys wearing red stilettoes, and certainly not like a senior pastor of a 110-year-old historic church. Every once in a while, I'll look in the mirror while I'm carefully applying my makeup and laugh out loud, "I'm a senior pastor!"

Not only do I not look the part, but I don't always *feel the part*. At the entrance to our church is a wall of pictures of those who have pastored the church in its 110-plus years. All of them are middle-aged white males except for one. I often jokingly sing the old Sesame Street song in my head while walking past the wall of pictures, "One of these pastors doesn't look like the others!" I don't necessarily look the part, and I often don't always feel like I am acting the stereotypical part, but that's okay.

THE DOUBLE-EDGED SWORD

On the other hand, the nurturing and emotive woman is exactly the stereotype associated with females. The issue is not so much that I am nurturing and maternal; rather, it's not often that you see a nurturing and maternal pastor. I have had conversations with many male pastors who lean more toward the nurturing side, and they too recognize it's not the norm (although wonderful!). Some of my male pastor friends have confessed a sense of marginalization by the high-powered alpha-male type pastors. They too feel unwelcome at the table. Not too long ago, a former campus minister and now pastor commented on the tension of fitting into gender stereotypes. After sharing an article I wrote on living outside of the senior pastor norm, he confessed, "I'm a middle-aged Asian American pastor leading a multiethnic church. So much of what you said applies to me as well." It's true, sometimes when women step out of the nurturing posture, that causes discomfort for some, and at times when men step into a nurturing posture, it too pushes the norm.

The opposite is the same too. I'll never forget Kat, a junior high campus minister for a parachurch organization outside of Chicago. She wasn't exactly the norm for women, and it was beautiful. She remained single as a campus minister, she preferred baseball caps and jerseys for clothing, she enjoyed four-wheeling and sporting events, and she could command a room of junior high boys unlike anyone I'd ever seen. She was a playful youth minister, and it wasn't uncommon to see her playing hoops in her long, mesh shorts and oversized T-shirt. Her playful spirit, her passion for Jesus, and her contagious energy made her the perfect campus minister with one of the fastest-growing programs in the country. She may not have fit the gender mold for some, but I thank God for my friend. She is one of the best junior high campus ministers I've ever met.

The point is this: there should be no mold! Let's face it, culture is a powerful machine, and many of us don't realize that the way we think, the way we view one another, and the constructs we place one another in are birthed out of cultural stereotypes. Undoing stereotypes is difficult, and it most certainly cannot happen without acknowledgment and intentionality. Stereotypes, of course, aren't just a phenomenon that women have to deal with; rather, stereotypes are wrapped up in generations, race, location, and more. Sheryl Sandberg notes,

> Decades of social science studies have confirmed . . . we evaluate people based on stereotypes (gender, race, nationality, and age, among others). Our stereotype of men holds that they are providers, decisive, and driven. Our stereotype of women holds that they are caregivers, sensitive, and communal. Because we characterize men and women in opposition to each other, professional

achievement and all the traits associated with it get placed in the male column. [2]

Due to stereotypes, women are all too often sidelined in the body of Christ. When a woman functions outside of the boundaries of the generally embraced stereotype, it often causes discomfort for those around her. Then when a woman steps into a typically male-dominated role, she is told she is acting like a man. This, of course, is an issue seen outside of the body of Christ. During the 2016 Olympics, female Olympians were smashing world records and raking in gold medals like it was their job. But as a *Huffington Post* article noted, their successes were often attributed to men.[3] When Katie Ledecky smashed a world record, it was tweeted that she *swam like a man*. And when Hungarian swimmer Katinka Hosszú broke the world record and won a gold medal, NBC reported that her husband was "the man responsible."[4] Sandberg also notes that "We're aware that when a woman acts forcefully or competitively, she's deviating from expected behavior. If a woman pushes to get the job done, if she's highly competent, if she focuses on results rather than on pleasing others, she's acting like a man. And if she acts like a man, people dislike her."[5]

These are often confusing narratives to women as they navigate leading in environments where gender stereotypes are most enforced. When I was a teenager and just starting to get involved in my local church, I never once met a woman preacher (although I am hopeful a shift is happening). But I met plenty of godly women in the church who loved to use their gifts by baking, arranging church potlucks, taking notes in the Sunday school classes, supporting pastors in administrative assistant roles, organize baby and bridal showers, playing the piano, writing cards, and organizing the children's ministry. And while all of these things are needed and so important in the local church, none of them excited me. I didn't go to bed at night dreaming of taking notes in a meeting or Sunday school class; while I love children, I didn't wake up in the morning thinking of ways to develop a Sunday school lesson; while I think organizing showers, potlucks, and all things that create community are needed, that's not what my dreams were made of. Rather, I was like the little girl on the playground who sat on the sidelines watching all the boys play dodgeball and wanting to join. When our male pastors got up to preach, I wanted to preach; when our male youth pastors led retreats, I wanted to lead retreats; when our male pastors got up to pray, I wanted to pray. No wonder it was hard for me to imagine what it might look like for me to teach, preach, and lead. I didn't fit the typical gender-stereotyped box, not even close.

Breaking through these gender stereotypes is a double-edged sword, however. When a woman is seen as trying to break through some of these molds, she is seen as being out of place, overstepping, self-promoting, or aggressive. Jackie Roese notes that these types of concerns for women are real. "Women are afraid they will be marked as feminists, B-words, man-usurpers. So they hold back, or worse yet, hold off entirely."[6] Throughout the years, I have been told dozens of times to be sure that I don't "lead like a man." While I recognize I am a woman and I can only lead like a woman (and we will talk more about this later), I was never sure what people meant when they cautioned me to not lead like a man. Did it mean that I couldn't be assertive or direct? Did it mean that I couldn't be ambitious and motivated? Did it mean that I couldn't be courageous and confident? These questions often swirled through my mind when I received this sort of advice.

No wonder women often don't speak up in meetings, and when they do we hear it couched in phrases such as "I'm just thinking out loud here" or "This might be a bad idea" or "I could be wrong" or "I was just thinking that we could maybe just . . ." Somehow by cushioning our words in these ways we think that just maybe the point we desire to get across will be easily embraced.

SMASHING THE GENDER MOLD:
DEBORAH, A WOMAN WITH PROWESS

In Deborah's day, patriarchy was no doubt the backdrop for these women's stories. And although some of the patriarchal greats like Abraham, Moses, and David are central to the story of Israel, Deborah's story leaps from the pages of the Old Testament because her story is critical to the people of God. She was fierce and fearless in every sense of these words. She was a prophet (Judg 4:4) and a judge (or leader). I love the way Scot McKnight expounds on her résumé:

Deborah was, to use modern analogies, the president, the pope, and Rambo all bundled up in one female body! . . . When the Bible says she was "leading" Israel, it uses the term for the *judge* of Israel. She was to her generation as Moses was to his. The word translated "judged" (*shapat*) combines the ideas of "national leadership," "judicial decisions," and "political, military savior." If we ask what did women do, and we ask this question of Deborah, we learn that women could speak for God as a prophet, render decisions in a law court as a judge, exercise leadership over the entire spiritual-social Israel, and be a military commander who brought Israel to victory. To use other terms, she led the nation spiritually, musically, legally, politically, and militarily. Let us not pretend her tasks were social and secular; Deborah was a woman leader of the entire people of God.[7]

Even with a brief reading of Judges 4, there can be no doubt that if there was any sort of patriarchal backdrop to the story of Israel, Deborah shattered it. Barak, a military commander, was so confident in her leadership and skills that he agreed to lead his troops only as long as Deborah went with him. When the time came, Deborah not only went with Barak but she also emboldened him to lead the troops: "Then Deborah said to Barak, 'Go! This is the day the LORD has given Sisera into your hands. Has not the LORD gone ahead of you?'" (Judg 4:14). And at Deborah's emboldening command, Barak went. I was sixteen years old when I first read Deborah's story, and I was completely enamored of her boldness, her prowess, and her lioness heart. She, no doubt, broke any mold that might have been in place, and her counterpart, Barak, embraced her God-given role.

DEBORAH WAS AN EMBOLDENED WOMAN

Deborah led the people of Israel, and following her victory she called the people of God to turn their hearts to God in a posture of worship—something a prophet would do. Singing in the age of the Old Testament was often tied to prophecy.[8] Read a little further and we discover that Deborah's prowess and ability to break through molds came not from within herself, but she was emboldened by the God of Israel. Take a moment and notice the words in italics and notice that Deborah was indeed *emboldened*.

"When the princes in Israel take the lead,
> when the people willingly offer themselves—
> *praise the LORD!*

"Hear this, you kings! Listen, you rulers!
> I, even I, will sing to the LORD;
> *I will praise the Lord, the God of Israel, in song.*

"*When you, LORD, went out from Seir,*
> *when you marched from the land of Edom,*
the earth shook, the heavens poured,
> *the clouds poured down water.*
The mountains quaked before the LORD, the One of Sinai,
> *before the LORD, the God of Israel. . . .*

"*Villagers in Israel would not fight;*
> *they held back until I, Deborah, arose,*
> *until I arose, a mother in Israel. . . .*
My heart is with Israel's princes,
> *with the willing volunteers among the people.*
> *Praise the Lord! . . .*

"'*Wake up, wake up, Deborah!*
> *Wake up, wake up, break out in song!*

Arise, Barak!
>   Take captive your captives, son of Abinoam.' . . .

"The princes of Issachar were with Deborah;
>   yes, Issachar was with Barak,
>   sent under his command into the valley. . . .
Gilead stayed beyond the Jordan.
>   And Dan, why did he linger by the ships?
Asher remained on the coast
>   and stayed in his coves.
The people of Zebulun risked their very lives;
>   so did Naphtali on the terraced fields.

"Kings came, they fought,
>   the kings of Canaan fought. . . .

"*So may all your enemies perish, LORD!*
>   *But may all who love you be like the sun*
>   *when it rises in its strength.*"
Then the land had peace forty years.
>   (Judg 5:2-31, emphasis added)

Deborah absolutely shattered the gender molds of her day. But her source and her strength came from a supernatural place, an intense love, passion, and belief in the Lord her God. It didn't matter if she was serving in a role that women didn't normally serve, she fearlessly went for it anyway with an abiding love for the Lord her God, who emboldened her to lead the people of Israel to victory.

Forcing women into gender stereotypes might be one of the greatest hindrances that sideline *even gifted* women in the body of Christ. But there is a lesson for all of us in Deborah and Barak's story. Deborah clearly had a divinely inspired imagination for her role among the people of God, which was supernaturally inspired, and Barak freely embraced her role. From the beginning and all the way to the end, Deborah's eyes and allegiance remained on her Lord, and this posture shaped her as a leader. Gender molds are real, no doubt, and I lament all the ways they have sidelined women in the body of Christ. What would it look like for us to allow the Spirit to not only divinely inspire our roles but to supernaturally help our brothers embrace those roles?

LEAD IN A WAY ONLY YOU CAN LEAD

Knowing that our roles within the body of Christ are divinely inspired, women who lead, teach, preach, and use their gifts within the kingdom should look like a divine rainbow of diversity. Some might very well have an inspired imagination to teach, preach, and lead fearlessly like Deborah. Others might lead maternally. For me, both are true. Breaking through gender molds doesn't mean we have to throw away how we might be as women. The truth is, we are women, and that is what we embrace, not stereotypes. After I preached a sermon not too long ago, someone came up to me and said, "You are so amazing when you preach, and you are so anointed! When you preach, I don't even see you as a woman!" I have no doubt this individual meant well when he said this, but I was left feeling rather perplexed; would it be a bad thing, then, if he saw me *as a woman* when I preached? I, for one, am glad I'm a *woman* who preaches, and I'm not ashamed to let that shine. In fact, it shines in all sorts of ways.

We aren't genderless, and there is something so mysterious about the gender identity that I so often have a difficult time wrapping my brain around. My gender identity, no doubt, is biological, it is shaped by culture, and it is part of God's paintbrush in creation. With that being said, there are times when I think I lead differently from anything I have observed from my male counterparts. Often, when I am sitting with one of our staff pastors going through a difficult time, something within me lights up that might look a little maternal. In all seriousness, I sometimes want to tell them to get comfy on the couch while I make them hot soup and warm chocolate chip cookies, and then we can cry together about their bad day! While I've never done that, I've learned to embrace the mysterious maternal nature deeply imbedded in the way I lead. I've never seen my male counterparts sit and cry with a staff member when they've had a bad day, but I've learned to embrace that this is how I sometimes lead. My sermon illustrations are often laced with maternal imagery, and I've learned to embrace the fact that my preaching leans in that direction. My leadership style tends to be less direct and more collaborative, and that is also okay. Breaking gender molds, you see, doesn't mean we move from leading one way to another; rather, it means we are free to lead in the only way that we can lead. Be you, dear sister.

KINGDOM WOMEN ARE DIVERSE

We are kingdom women, and we are diverse. We have short hair and we have long hair; dirt is under our fingernails from toiling under the sun, and our fingernails are nicely manicured with pink nail polish; we stay at home with the children, care for our husbands, and support their careers, but we also choose to wear blue pantsuits and pastor churches. We wear yoga pants, leggings, mom jeans, cargo shorts, long skirts, and daisy dukes. You see, our femininity is not rooted in ideology or cultural norms but in our humanity, which *is firmly rooted in the humanity of Christ*. The life, death, resurrection, and ascension of King Jesus informs our identities. We sometimes bear children and sometimes don't, but childbearing *isn't our identity*; instead, our identities are ordered in the saving and transforming activity of the triune God.

Our lives are *firmly rooted in Jesus Christ*, and we are emboldened by the empowering presence of the Spirit. The Spirit informs our decisions in the office, at home, behind a cashier's counter, and in our relationships; by the Spirit we are shaped into the *women we were created to be—biblical women, holy women, and daughters of the resurrection*. We are beautiful, strong, courageous, quiet, submissive, outspoken, tender, fierce, and emboldened.

We are kingdom women, and we are *in Christ*. When we gather together every week for prayer, praise, and Eucharist, the empowering presence of the Spirit is among us, and that is when we *shine*. Imagine the introverted church planter Ming-An, who although introverted is deeply relational and has the ability to meet the unchurched where they are. Imagine Jameelah, the gospel-singing and extroverted theologian. Imagine Dana, the women's director who is happily single and would rather be at a Cubs game than a craft party. Imagine Rosa, the nonprofit director who loves numbers and spreadsheets, and thereby attempts to help further the cause of social justice.

Kingdom women are diverse, you see. We have gifts to teach, preach, prophesy, serve, lead, and build. We are church planters, we are kitchen ladies, we are number crunchers, we are directors, and we are worship leaders. We are nurturing, we are assertive, we are maternal, and we are fierce. We are full of wisdom, and we are also new Christians. Many have tried to box us in or tell us who we *should be*, but when we look to Christ, we see cruciformity, love, grace, courage, and presence. Sure, try to box us in, but we are kingdom women, and we are diverse.

FOUR

OVERCOMING OPPOSITION

"THAT'S WONDERFUL that you have experienced such a strong sense of call, Tara Beth, but you must be mistaken, women can't be pastors," said a youth leader after I had just poured my heart out to him regarding a profound experience I had just had. He went on, "You could be a women's pastor or a children's pastor or a missionary, but not a senior pastor."[1]

That was the first of dozens of times I have heard something like this. So naturally, when I graduated from college and stepped into my first pastoral role, I thought the only challenge I would face as a woman in ministry was more of the same—someone expressing their belief that women couldn't pastor or teach or preach. Indeed, I've endured that conversation more times than I'd want to admit, but to my surprise that hasn't been the only challenge.

I am not saying that women pastors are the only ones who face challenges; of course, men have their own set of challenges. But when I stepped into my youth pastor role in upstate New York in 2004, I was clueless that I would have to worry about things such as what I would wear on a Sunday morning. You see, clothes for women are much more of a balancing act; is it fitted, but not too fitted; professional, but still modest? And it is not uncommon for me to receive reactions regarding my clothing choices. I never considered that I would have to be concerned about my voice being too high pitched for the listening ear, and this too is something I have been warned about on more than one occasion. I never thought I would be accused of leading like a man after responding to a situation with assertiveness and directness. And perhaps I was naive, but I hardly considered the opposition I would face simply for being a female pastor—that is, until I experienced it. Navigating the waters as a woman in ministry is both exhilarating and challenging, and every context has its own unique encounters. If you are a woman leading in the body of Christ, more than likely you have tasted opposition.

OPPOSITION HAPPENS

It was another Sunday morning and another sermon. I anxiously and prayerfully sat as I clenched my leather preaching Bible in the front pew. I was only minutes away from preaching a sermon before a congregation I loved, knew, and cared for. A rainbow of emotions flooded my mind, body, and soul. My heart raced. It was the same swirl of emotions that always seems to overtake my heart before preaching—a tiny bit of fear, but enough courage from the Spirit to get me up there. I could only rely on what the Spirit would do within the next few minutes.

This particular Sunday presented a different challenge. In the middle of the sermon, a middle-aged man (who I'll call Joe) made his way down the center aisle and sat in the front row and listened intently; I almost thought he was going to stop me from preaching. As the service ended, Joe quickly jumped to his feet and handed me a sheet of paper with several Scriptures written in red ink. "This is the Holy Word of God," he said. "I can't argue with God." When I looked at the paper I noticed that it was saturated in passages similar to 1 Timothy 2:12. "Since you are a woman, you have no business preaching and teaching," Joe said. As I attempted to gently walk Joe through some of the passages, I realized I was getting nowhere, and he only got angrier. Joe's words were piercing and left me feeling wounded, which I have felt other times through emails, letters, and phone calls similar in content.

Opposition shows up in many shapes, forms, and sizes. It has shown up in the form of a youth pastor explaining to me that God would only call me into ministry if men didn't step up to *their* calling *first*, or a classmate in Bible school explaining why I can't be a *lead* pastor, or a friend sending me a three-thousand-word Facebook message as to why he "wishes" he could be excited for me serving in his church, but cannot because I am "blaspheming the name of God as a woman preacher," or a denominational leader who ignores my emails and phone calls for six-plus months, or even a friend standing in my kitchen after eating a meal explaining to me that he is not comfortable with a woman preacher. Oh, I could go on and on. Opposition can come in the form of an angry email, red letters on a paper, or blatant ignoring.

WHEN OPPOSITION COMES, THERE IS ALWAYS A CROSSROADS

Because I serve as a senior pastor, some have called me a "trailblazer for shattering the glass ceiling," or as blogger Jory

Micah often says, "shattering the glass steeple."[2] Many think that my accepting a call to this position means I have arrived and gender isn't a conversation at the church. However, as much as I would like to say that we have "arrived" at PazNaz since we have called and affirmed a female pastor, we have not. In the early days, there was hardly a week that gender didn't come up, or hardly a week when I wouldn't hear a story of someone deciding to leave the church because they "just can't do a female pastor." While the majority of our community is excited and affirming, there are very loud voices that are not.

I met with a woman in my office after reaching out to her upon learning that her family was leaving the church. I was surprised to learn they were leaving, because it was a family I knew and loved. Whenever someone decides to leave the church, it is just about as painful as any sort of relational breakup. I often experience a day or two of grief followed by some tears. But this meeting was unique. As we sat in my office on that sunny December afternoon, she shared that she and her children were leaving the church because she decided that a female pastor was a "liberal view."

"I'm sorry," she said, "but I firmly believe that the role of the senior pastor needs to be a man. But please don't take this personally." As I sat there and listened to her explain her position, I'd like to say I didn't take it personally, but I did. Every word of it hurt deeply. About a week leading up to that day, I had heard several other stories of folks deciding to leave because they had come to similar conclusions.

I wish I could say I didn't take any of those comments personally. I wish I could say it didn't hurt. But it does, and I do take it personally. I left my office that night and sat in a grocery store parking lot and wept with my face buried in my steering wheel. I wept, I prayed, and I cried out, "How long, O Lord, will the bride of Christ continue to limp along?" I came home and my husband and I together lamented.

Lament and grief are normal emotions in the face of opposition. Feelings of anger are normal. But as I lead this church that I love so very dearly, I always have to ask myself, *What am I leading with?* You see, I could make it my personal mission to prove to my opponents *how wrong they are*; I could flood my Facebook wall with blogs and articles on women in ministry; I could do a five-part preaching series on why women should be in the pulpit; I could get angry, shout, yell, and be bitter. In every situation, I am praying for wisdom, discernment, grace, and to be led by the Spirit. Yes, I am absolutely tired of gender being a conversation, but leading with this as an agenda will likely set our congregation back.

Leading with anger and bitterness won't fill a room of eager listeners wanting to learn more, but it will likely scare them away. But taking the posture of Jesus—that is, loving my opponents, praying for them, and serving them—will likely advance the message more than it will hinder it. Arguing with my opponents with a chip on my shoulder will turn them away even more.

There was another time I started to hear rumblings of a family who thought I wasn't fit for the job because both my age and gender. At one point I even heard the family actually say they "hated" me. That statement took several days to get over, and I certainly licked my wounds on that one. But after much prayer and conversation, my husband and I decided to pursue this family with the love and hospitality of Jesus. So we invited them over for a meal at our home, much like we do with many families. Our table has become a place where Jeff and I have been able to find common ground, show the hospitality of Jesus, and be conduits of love and grace.

Every time I come face-to-face with an "opponent," I reach a crossroads: bitterness and anger eventually will become my banner, or I can simply *preach on, teach on, lead on, serve on.* I could argue and get combative. (Believe me, the urge is there every time!) I could shake my fist, cry, and tell them all why I think they are wrong. I could shout the names Junia, Mary, Deborah, Esther, Phoebe, and Priscilla. I could yell and tell them that they will someday be held accountable before God for hindering gifted, Spirit-filled, and called women from using their gifts to edify the body of Christ. However, the moment I decide to let anger and bitterness seep into the very depths of my being is the moment I lose sight of what I was called to do in the first place. Resentment and animosity become my starting points instead of leaning into the empowering presence of the Spirit and allowing grace and love to be the banner under which I serve, lead, shepherd, teach, and preach.

JESUS' TEACHING ON ANGER

When reading the vision Jesus illustrated in the Sermon on the Mount, we are pushed by the words of Jesus to *not* choose anger. Rather, we are called to love recklessly. In a section of the Sermon known as the "Antitheses" (Mt 5:17-48), Jesus demands more of his followers by pushing them to embody his vision for the new kingdom community. Jesus' teachings are not mere practical advice for beneficial living, but prophetic proclamations made of the coming and already present kingdom of God.

Jesus began his first antithesis with a shock to his listeners by pushing them to understand the severity of anger in the kingdom community.

> You have heard that it was said to the people long ago, "You shall not murder, and anyone who murders will be subject to judgment." But I tell you that anyone who is angry with a brother or sister will be subject to judgment. Again, anyone who says to a brother or sister, "Raca," is answerable to the court. And anyone who says, "You fool!" will be in danger of the fire of hell. (Mt 15:21-22)

The Jewish listener would have known murder was against Jewish law, but Jesus sets a new ethical code for the already-but-not-yet kingdom community. The future kingdom of God in Revelation 21 illustrates that anger will be no more. *Love, grace,* and *unity* will permeate the people of God. When women choose love, grace, and forgiveness in the face of resistance, we give the world a foretaste of the kingdom of God.

As followers of Jesus, we are called to live into this kingdom reality here and now—the kingdom reality that practices peace, presence, love, and grace over and against anger and bitterness. When we live as daughters of peace and love, others around us might notice. They might even stop in their tracks in order to peer into the church and get a foretaste of this kingdom reality alive within us. I long for that. I long for the world to see the loving power of the Holy Spirit unleashed in women! I long to see the loving power of the Holy Spirit unleashed in you and in me.

The Holy Spirit, not anger, empowers me to serve the church. My calling, not anger, keeps me in the pulpit in the face of opposition. The cross puts to death the anger, bitterness, rage, and malice in my heart. Grace, not the enemy, enables me to look at opponents as children of God. Jesus, the King who sits on the throne, reminds me that my calling is not mine to behold or control. The future kingdom of God calls me to live a life of peace and presence, even when I am told that I cannot preach. The faithfulness of King Jesus drives me to forgive and love subversively, even when it hurts.

As daughters of the kingdom, we choose love, grace, and forgiveness, not bitterness and anger. Bitterness draws hard lines in the sand; love is hospitable. Bitterness paralyzes; forgiveness empowers. Anger and hatred punish; love forgives. Bitterness hoards; grace is generous. Hatred excludes; forgiveness includes. Anger hurts our neighbors; love heals our neighbors.

BITTERNESS ONLY HINDERS

In ministry, leaders occasionally encounter people who believe leaders can do no wrong. However, other people think leaders can do nothing right. Several years ago a woman in our church thought I could do no right (let's call her Jan). To make a long and complicated story short, when I came into the church, I wasn't the pastor Jan wanted. There was a young man who applied for the job and happened to be very close with Jan; so naturally Jan was quite upset that I came instead of her friend.

From day one she opposed me, and she let me know this not only by her body language whenever I entered a room, but also by the lengthy and angry emails she sent to me on a regular basis. Her emails were some of the most painful and hurtful I've ever read in my entire life. It was as though she knew my insecurities and vulnerabilities well and would go out of her way to attack them.

Bitterness is a funny thing; it lurks in the darkest corners of our hearts: it simmers, it boils, and when we least expect it, it seeps into everything. It affects the way we lead, the way we pray, our perspective, and the way we minister. Bitterness tells us that *we are the victim*, and it paralyzes love and joy and goodness and gentleness. At least, this is how it was for me. Whenever I would receive an email from Jan, I would read it not just once but dozens of times, and then I would go home and talk about it all night with my husband, and would think about it through the night. Whenever I saw her in church, my thoughts toward her were not peaceful; rather, they were filled with anger, rage, and hatred. That's what bitterness does. In those days, I chose to be led by anger, bitterness, and rage instead of being led by the goodness and grace of the Spirit.

It's taken me years to know when bitterness is creeping at my door when I'm facing opposition. It's taken me years to turn toward the peace and goodness of Christ over and against bitterness. It's taken me years to recognize that moving along is what I am called to do.

There's a notion that as women we *should* be angry when we aren't given equal opportunity, particularly in the pulpit. Some say that women have been placed in a cultural construct where anger is improper and not ladylike, therefore, we should fight against that construct. We have the *right* to be angry. Some say that anger is the best response when it comes to injustice, opposition, and oppression. Jesus, after all, got angry.

There are times when I do feel angry when I think about the injustices women around the world have endured. There are times my stomach is in knots when I watch a clip of a prominent pastor talk about how women have no place of leadership in the church. And I've often wondered if I would be able to sit through a sermon from this particular pastor.

But I don't want to *choose* anger as my go-to response and use it as my banner. I'm not sure how to decouple anger from not only a defensive posture but also bitterness. I'm not sure how to get angry without dwelling on it, even obsessing over it. I'm not sure how to get angry and *not* act on my anger.

TIPS FOR SURVIVAL

I sat like a wet noodle at the table in a cold room. My tears were falling so fast that my tissue was not able to keep them from falling to the table. "It's just so hard, you know? Men never have to deal with the stuff that women have to deal with. They never have to hear the comments we hear; they never have to worry about the things we have to worry about. It's just not fair." My mentor looked at me with compassionate eyes in a sweet moment of empathy, but then sternly said, "It is hard dear, but how thick is your skin? Because if you're going to be a woman in ministry, you have to have thick skin."

She was right. At times it is so easy to obsess over the opposition we face, the things we hear, or our lack of opportunities.

But I can either choose to allow these things to defeat me and tear me down, or I can move from surviving to thriving. I don't know about you, dear sister, but I want to thrive. So the following are a few tips on how we can move from surviving to thriving.

Know your argument. In ministry, difficult conversations often happen when we least expect them and usually when we least desire them. While I was transitioning from my church in Chicago to PazNaz, my dear, sweet church in Chicago threw me the most beautiful going-away party between services. I stood among friends as we had cake and punch, and many people came to greet me and give me their love, wishes, and prayers. Person after person came through the long line in the commons area and offered me encouragement, love, prayers, cards, and gifts. Eventually, a man made his way through the line to me and began the conversation like this: "What makes you think you can go and be a senior pastor? Scripture is *clear* you have no authority or right to be a senior pastor. It's fine that you teach and preach to women, but never to men."

I stood there dumbfounded, confused, and speechless. I can't even remember what I said to this man, but I blubbered my way through some sort of response. I then realized that I needed to rehearse a noncombative response for situations like this. If the situation is appropriate, know your argument, know the right questions to ask, have your four-minute elevator speech, and be prepared. I've now learned from Scot McKnight to respond with WDWD?—What did women do?[3] A simple way to respond is to rehearse with the person the female leaders, apostles, and preachers in the Bible. Then end with the statement, "We have to read the Bible in light of the entire story of God. Women played significant roles. Perhaps some of the tough passages are descriptive of the context and more of a backdrop to what was happening rather than prescriptive."

Relax, it's not a battle. You won't convince them here and now. Often, when we are approached by those who oppose our ministry, the knee-jerk response is to get in battle mode. Maybe I'm the only one who at times gets defensive in situations like this, but it's not uncommon for me to feel angry and be tempted to respond in a snarky tone. It is difficult to not take things personally—this might be one of my greatest struggles—but within the body of Christ we are not in a battle. Instead, we are edifying, we are shepherding, we are leading, we are teaching, and we are admonishing—even those who might be opposed to us. Furthermore, we usually won't convince someone who is opposed to women in ministry in one conversation. Often it takes folks significant time to process, read, listen, and pray before coming to the same conclusions that you have come to years ago. So lay down your weapons, dear sister; the folks we are talking with are still our brothers and sisters in Christ. Give them time, lead them when you can, teach them when you can, edify them when you can, but trust the work of the Spirit. And as hard as it might be to remember, Jesus died for them too.

Pray for compassion. I am always in awe of Stephen, the martyr in the book of Acts. In Acts 7:55, we learn that Stephen was a man full of the Holy Spirit. After preaching one of the most glorious sermons recorded in the New Testament, Stephen was dragged outside the city and stoned by his opposers. As the stones were being thrown at him, as he felt the piercing pain on his skin, Stephen prayed, "Lord, do not hold this sin against them" (Acts 7:60). Stephen's prayer counters how we often respond to opposition. But Stephen's prayer came from a place of compassion, love, and being able to see people the way Jesus saw them—even his opponents. Not too long ago I began to pray for the Spirit to give me a heart of compassion and love for those who, due to my gender, oppose me as a pastor. The Spirit is always faithful, and when we pray for such things, transformation happens.

Eyes on King Jesus. When Jeff and I moved to Chicagoland, I had big dreams and visions to be a part of a church-planting movement in the city. So when we moved there, I immediately began calling my denominational leader to let him know my interest to be involved in the planting movement. In fact, many of my close friends were being commissioned. I spent several months making phone calls and sending emails to our denominational office. I left voicemails. I sent emails. I poured out my heart. I shared my excitement. I prayed. I longed. I waited. And in my longing, in my calling, in my excitement, I waited but never heard a word back. In fact, I lived in our region for six years before a single opportunity came from my denomination. I watched friend after friend accept exciting ministry opportunities, but I eventually had to pursue an opportunity at another great church—outside my tribe. But whenever I would scroll through my newsfeed looking at pictures of my friends' exciting ministry opportunities, bitterness would begin to knock on the door. I would whisper to the Lord, "Lord, it's just not fair!"

In John 21, we catch a glimpse of an intimate conversation between Jesus and Peter. As Peter and Jesus slowly walk along the shore, Jesus cuts to the heart and asks, "Do you love me?" After Jesus asks Peter this question three times and Peter responds, Jesus commissions him with a fresh challenge and calling: feed lambs and sheep. Something profound happens on those shores; Jesus trusts Peter to participate in the ministry of shepherding. Peter then learns that by participating in the ministry of Jesus, his task would be complete by laying down his own life.

But then Peter's mind begins to swirl with questions and insecurities. He looks over his shoulder to see the "beloved disciple" in view and asks Jesus, "What about him?" (Jn 21:21). Jesus reminds Peter that his task is not to worry about others' callings; rather, Peter is to follow Jesus. *Jesus made no mistake in calling Peter to participate in the ministry of caring for his sheep.* In the book of Acts, we see Peter did exactly what he was commissioned to do—shepherd the sheep with his eye constantly on his King.

Our calling as proclaimers of the gospel and shepherds of the people of God is to follow Jesus wherever he leads. Ultimately, this calling rests under the authority of King Jesus, and at the end of the day, he is the one we follow. As I daily walk with Jesus, and as I participate in this incredible task of feeding his sheep, there are constant opportunities for me to look over my shoulder and ask, "What about him?" There are countless opportunities for me to say, "Not fair, Lord!" There are countless opportunities for me to choose bitterness. Truth be told, there are more than a few times I have wanted to throw a temper tantrum, shake my fist in the air and ask, "What *about* him, Jesus? How can this man (or this pastor) have such a fruitful ministry and limit *so many women from feeding your sheep? It's not fair!*" And in that moment the Spirit whispers, *"What about him? What's that got to do with you? Keep your eye on me, Tara Beth!"*

Frankly, sometimes it doesn't seem fair, and sometimes anger and bitterness get the best of me. But this most often happens when my eyes come off King Jesus. When I obsess over the situations that have brought opposition, the fruits are anger and bitterness. The apostle Paul was onto something when he said, "Finally, brothers and sisters, whatever is true, whatever is noble, whatever is right, whatever is pure, whatever is lovely, whatever is admirable—if anything is excellent or praiseworthy—think about such things" (Phil 4:8). And the wild thing about this passage is, Paul wrote this while living through some of the worst opposition of his life—he was *in chains*; talk about being sidelined! And yet, as Paul wrote from chains, he declared, "Rejoice in the Lord always. I will say it again: Rejoice!" (Phil 4:4). Not only did Paul's opposition cause him to rejoice, but it also emboldened him to preach the gospel, even from the sidelines! At the introduction of his letter he declares,

> Now I want you to know, brothers and sisters, that what has happened to me has actually served to advance the gospel. As a result, it has become clear throughout the whole palace guard and to everyone else that I am in chains for Christ. *And because of my chains, most of the*

brothers and sisters have become confident in the Lord and
dare all the more to proclaim the gospel without fear. (Phil
1:12-14, emphasis added)

Paul, in chains, was an emboldened proclaimer of the
gospel— without anger and full of joy. How was this possible?
Paul wasn't superhuman; he was a Spirit-filled human whose
eyes were on King Jesus. In Philippians 2, Paul urged others to
"have the same mindset as Christ" (Phil 2:5), and in Philippians
3 Paul reveals where his eyes are focused, "But one thing I do:
Forgetting what is behind and straining toward what is ahead,
I press on toward the goal to win the prize for which God has
called me heavenward in Christ Jesus" (Phil 3:13-14).

To be sure, Paul wasn't a fan of his opponents. In fact he
describes them like this: "Their destiny is destruction, their god
is their stomach, and their glory is in their shame. Their mind
is set on earthly things" (Phil 3:19). But Paul urges others to
follow his own example, living as a citizen of heaven (Phil 3:20).
In chains and completely sidelined, Paul's eyes stayed on the
King. He was empowered by the Spirit. Paul didn't lead with
anger and bitterness, but was led by the Spirit. I don't want to
lead out of anger and bitterness; I want to be a woman on
mission, emboldened by the Spirit, with my eyes on the King.

We are not the *ultimate authority* but simply a conduit of
God's grace, truth, and love under the reign of King Jesus.
When we are faithful to the task we have been called to, whether
it is preaching, leading, teaching, evangelizing, organizing, or
nurturing, hearts are transformed and the body of Christ is
edified. Opposition will happen. Sometimes you might not

notice, and sometimes it will cut deep—to the heart. But you have been created and called for such an incredible time as this. So, instead of allowing bitterness and anger to be the banner under which you lead, *preach on, teach on, lead on, move on with grace, love,* and in the *power of the Spirit.*

While these are survival tactics I have learned over the years, research also helps us navigate tough situations. The following are a few helpful tips:

1. Stay calm; don't react with your first angry instinct.
2. Listen to understand, not to argue.
3. Find common ground; listen hard for it.
4. State your case tactfully and in a winsome manner.
5. Don't attack the person with name calling or verbal shaming.
6. Avoid the blame game.
7. Ask the right kinds of questions.
8. Pick your battles.
9. Be creative.
10. Be confident.
11. Be humble.
12. Celebrate agreement.[4]

Remember "Joe" at the beginning of this chapter? Five days after my difficult conversation with him, he had a severe brain aneurism and almost lost his life. As a single man with hardly any family in town, Joe didn't have many people to visit him. Since our other pastor was on vacation, I was on hospital visit duty. Knowing that our last conversation had left me wounded, I struggled with the thought of visiting Joe. It was difficult to love Joe. As I arrived at the hospital, I stopped for a moment to whisper a prayer. I prayed for the Spirit to propel and impel me to love Joe with the same self-sacrificial love of God that Jesus talked about in the Sermon on the Mount.

When I walked into the room, I was overcome with sadness for Joe. I saw him slumped in a wheelchair with his head down, sadly staring at the floor. He sat alone and helpless; it hurt my heart. I had never before felt such loneliness and brokenness as I did when I looked at him that day.

I sat next to him, and he was well enough to know who I was and carry on a conversation. About halfway through the conversation, I placed my hand on his hand and said, "Joe, we've been praying for you at church, and we love you." As those words came out of my mouth, his body shook with emotion as he began to weep uncontrollably. At that moment, I knew I had meant it; I loved Joe. As a daughter of the kingdom of God, the Spirit had indeed propelled me and impelled me to love him with the indiscriminate love of the Father. That's what the living God can do in and through us: even in the darkest days of opposition, the Spirit turns our heart toward love and grace.

FIVE

AN EMBOLDENED SISTERHOOD

I WEPT AS CARLA AND I STOOD in the corner of the cold Sunday school room in the basement of an old church on the college campus of Olivet Nazarene University. She was there to speak to the four thousand-plus student body and then do a banquet for women in ministry.

Flashback to two hours before: I was exhausted, fried, and didn't even want to be there that day. It was over an hour drive just to get there, and taking a day off from ministry and school and being away from children was exhausting. But something in me told me I needed to be there to see and hear Carla speak. When she preached in chapel that day, she preached with authority, power, and boldness that I had rarely seen in a woman. After, I was afraid to approach her and assumed she had a million other women who wanted to talk to her, so I just watched her teach, preach, lead, and minister from afar.

In between chapel and the banquet, I was waiting in the hallway checking my cell phone when Carla made her way toward me. She seemed eager to greet me and said, "You're

Tara Beth Leach, our Nazarene minister on loan!" This was the beginning of the conversation that forever changed my life. You see, I was a passionate Wesleyan-Holiness gal serving outside of my own denomination. Doors of ministry had been flinging wide open for me and life couldn't have been more exciting. Writing and preaching opportunities had been coming my way left and right, but none from my own denomination.

As Carla and I walked toward the church where the banquet was being held, we made our way into the basement of the church. As we chatted, I began to pour my heart out to her. "Carla, I could not be more grateful for the opportunities that are coming my way. I *get* to preach Jesus, I *get* to write about Jesus. I am even being pursued by one of the largest churches in the country, but my own tribe hardly knows I exist." You see, in my own denomination many women are leaving for lack of opportunity. I was one of those women who was not serving in my own denomination due to lack of opportunity.

Carla cried with me, told me I wasn't alone, validated my feelings, offered wisdom, and shared some of her own story for hope and encouragement. After our conversation that day, I assumed I would never hear from her again. She was the president of a seminary, an author, a blogger, and an in-demand speaker for conferences and retreats. Carla was and is busy, and she could have very easily moved onto the next thing and forgotten about our conversation that day. But she didn't. Carla began to check in on me, send notes of encouragement, and *embolden me.*

Just about a month after our conversation in that cold Sunday school room, I got a phone call from Carla. "Tara Beth, are you open to talking to other churches about pastoring?" "Of course!" I told her. She shared with me that she frequently gets calls from churches who are looking for pastors, and she wanted to know if she could add my name to that list. At first I thought she was just feeling extra compassionate, but then she shared that she had been reading my work and watching my sermons online. "I really believe in you, Tara Beth." When I hung up the phone that day, I still didn't think anything would come of it—that is, until November 2015.

Carla called me on a blustery, cold afternoon in Chicago. "Tara Beth, I think I have a church that is interested in you." I listened to her talk about the church for about fifteen minutes and then she said, "Do you want to know what church I'm talking about?" "Of course," I said. "It's PazNaz." I must have been speechless, because after some time went by she said, "Are you there?" I knew PazNaz, but I never thought I'd pastor there. Carla then said, "Now don't get your hopes up, they are still in the beginning stages. But I want you to know that I really believe in you, Tara Beth." I gulped and eventually hung up the phone.

After six months of conversation, prayers, discernment, and interviews, I was installed as the senior pastor at PazNaz on May 22, 2016. Throughout the entire process, Carla walked with me, encouraged me, prayed for me, and always went out of her way to help me, which she still does to this day. Carla is a woman who emboldens women.

With very few women in ministry, it's been difficult for me to find mentors who "get" the challenges that women face on a regular basis. While I am grateful for all of the male mentors in my life—and almost all of them have been men—they will never fully understand the bumps, setbacks, and pushbacks women in ministry face. Here are just a few examples of things that my male mentors may not have experienced:

- Stress about clothing choices: Is it too tight? Too "feminine"? Too "masculine"? Too short? Inappropriate?

- Motherhood and ministry

- Navigating female friendships in ministry

- Working through gender-specific wounds: For example, hearing on a regular basis that someone "just can't be a *woman* leader/pastor/teacher/preacher," or hearing on a regular basis that someone is leaving a church because of the gender of the leader

- Navigating a lack of opportunities because of gender

- Navigating inappropriate or odd comments: "You are one hot pastor" or "When you were preaching I could only focus on your big, pregnant belly" or "Your hair is such a distraction, will you please get it under control?"

Many have been inspired by the amplification strategy adopted by female White House staff under President Obama. When President Obama began serving as president, women there were outnumbered and unheard in most meetings. So the women rallied together and came up with an approach called "amplification" by creating spaces for women's voices at the table. If a woman made a point, other women in the room would repeat it while giving praise to the one who made the point. Men and women could begin practicing this *now* to amplify and highlight the voice of women.

Although there are very few female leaders within the church, women must work together; women must be willing to mentor, encourage, amplify, help, walk with, pray for, and embolden other women within the body of Christ. Here are some concrete actions we can take to embolden one another:

- Prayerfully look for and pursue women who you might be able to mentor in your local church or place of ministry.

- If you observe a gift that has potential to grow in another woman, point it out.

- When another woman gets an opportunity in your church or place of ministry (even if it's an opportunity you would love to have), root her on, cheer for her, and encourage her.

- When possible, open doors for other women. For example, if you have the ability to schedule women in a teaching rotation, be generous.

- Train, mentor, and encourage women who have gifts similar to yours. If you are a gifted teacher, be generous with your knowledge. Get creative! Perhaps start a class in your church to train women how to teach the Bible.

- If you see a woman experiencing setbacks or roadblocks in her ministry journey, be empathetic, listen, and pray with her.

- In your church or place of ministry, make it a goal to be the biggest cheerleader for other women in your midst.

ONE SEAT AT THE TABLE

Sometimes, when women should be *emboldening one another* and working hard to be on the same team, the opposite happens. Sometimes, women hold back or even injure one another. Perhaps it's because of the notion that there is only *one seat* at the table. I have two brothers close in age, and growing up we used to fight over a lot of things. But nothing caused a sibling brawl quite like a fight over riding "shotgun," also known as the front seat of the car. Only one could ride shotgun, but there were three of us. Anytime we would leave the house, all of us would run to the front of the car—pushing and shoving, and sometimes tackling each other too as we yelled, "My turn for shotgun!" Among women there seems to be the notion that if a seat at the table ever opens up, there will only be room for one. So we push, shove, get jealous, and say hurtful things, all the while forgetting we are on the same team and thus hindering the mission.

I wish I could say tokenism is gone in the body of Christ, but sadly it is not. Tokenism isn't just a setback within the body of Christ, it's a prevailing problem, as it is in corporate America. The *Harvard Business Review* published a study that found having one woman in a job pool does not increase the likelihood of her being hired. But when there are two female candidates, the probability dramatically increases.[1] In other words, tokenism is just that: tokenism. Having one seat at the table doesn't change the culture of an organization, but when more women's voices are welcomed, the tide begins to change.

Not too long ago I received an email asking if I would be willing and available to speak at a major Christian conference. I was excited, no doubt, and honored to be considered. About two months later I received another email stating that they only wanted *one* female speaker, and I had been "knocked out of the running." Several years ago I had the opportunity to hire a junior high pastor while I was the senior high pastor. Again, I was told that I could not hire a female youth pastor because we couldn't have *two* female pastors. (However, before coming to that church there had been an *all-male staff*.) These are just two examples of the many times I have encountered tokenism, and it is, no doubt, discouraging. Sheryl Sandberg notes this same mentality in the corporate world: "Unfortunately, this 'there can only be one' attitude still lingers today. It makes no sense for women to feel that we are competing against one another anymore, but some still do."[2] Sadly, as long as tokenism exists in churches, I fear that women will continue to compete against one another for a seat at the table.

Even where there is tokenism, women must be *for one another*; women must *embolden* one another. Natasha Sistrunk Robinson writes,

> Then there's the top-down approach. In publishing and blogging, we talk about "platform." For leaders, Jenni Catron calls it "clout." Whatever the term, people in positions of power have the opportunity to steward their influence. They can keep the issue of diversity at the forefront of their organizational priorities and conversations. Beyond that, they can choose to feature the voices of women and racial minorities.
>
> This stewardship is important for our churches and organizations, but especially for conferences—where people look to the lineups to see who they should be listening or paying attention to. Last year's Nines conference had over

30,000 viewers, and there was much promotion going on during the presentations at this year's conference. In addition to the stage, there is a lot of book and product placements at major conferences. These events encourage an embrace of new voices in our reading, organizations, and other areas of life. Additionally, consistently championing diverse voices will likely increase more diverse attendance and viewership over time, which will result in broader conversations and just actions across the board.[3]

One of my favorite gatherings to attend every other year is the Missio Alliance national conference. I am always blessed by the very diverse speaker lineup, and I am constantly challenged by the variety of perspectives on the platform. I often get a glimpse of the fullness of God's kingdom. I am thankful for organizations like Missio Alliance, the Justice Conference, and Community Christian Development Association, who are leading the way.

MEAN GIRLS

Several years ago I endeavored to write a Bible study on the Sermon on the Mount for several hundred women. The Bible study was a labor of love, passion, and joy. When the books arrived for us to distribute to our three hundred or so women, it felt like Christmas morning. Almost all of the women were just as excited as I was because many were on the editing and writing journey with me. But one woman in particular thought it was deplorable that I would even consider writing a Bible study. I was dumbfounded by her anger, and yet she raked me over the coals with email after email for writing a Bible study. To her it was arrogant, and I was way too young to do such a thing. Although my predecessors were authors and had written their own Bible studies, to this woman thirty-four was way too young to pen a Bible study, and I was perceived as arrogant.

Being a woman in ministry, I would think that my biggest advocates most often would be women and my biggest naysayers most often would be men. However, this is not always the case. Nancy Beach is sadly right: "Just as adolescents can be *mean girls*, grown-ups can turn into *mean women* who subtly —or not so subtly—undermine, judge, and criticize the choices of other women they worship next to on Sunday mornings."[4] Jamie Ostrov, a professor, psychologist, and researcher, discovered that triangulation behavior begins as early as age three: "Aggressive behavior in girls from ages 3 to 5 tends to be more direct, but by early adolescence it starts becoming much more covert," Ostrov says. He notes that girls who are victims of this behavior are more likely to demonstrate symptoms like depression, anxiety, and academic problems.[5]

Sadly, all too often this "mean girls" behavior still exists within the bride of Christ. More often than not, some of the most hurtful and painful things said to me as a woman in ministry have been from women. Women are all too often the most critical of one another rather than cheering one another on. If women continue to push, shove, criticize, and fight for seats at the table, perhaps there will always only be one seat at the table.

When I began serving as a staff pastor at a church in Oak Brook, Illinois, there was a young, tenacious, and gifted female pastor on staff, Tracey Bianchi. Tracey was a well-known and

gifted author, speaker, preacher, and pastor. She has stood on
the main stage of several Christian conferences, yet you would
never know it when meeting her. She is generous, present, gracious, and kind with every person she meets. When I came on
staff, I filled her old position because she was moving into a
teaching and worship position in the church. Before coming on
board, Tracey was the only female teaching pastor, but with me,
there were now two of us. Tracey could have very well sized me
up and seen me as a threat, but instead Tracey was my biggest
cheerleader while I was on staff there. There were many times
when we prayed together, cried together, commiserated together, and hoped for the fullness of the kingdom together.
Whenever I had a new writing opportunity, Tracey flooded me
with encouragement, and if I was preaching, she would check
in with me, send me texts of encouragement, and be the first
to cheer me on. Tracey emboldens women.

I am reminded of the friendship between Mary and Elizabeth. Mary, the soon-to-be mother of not just any bouncing
baby boy, but the Messiah himself, enters the home of another
pregnant woman, Elizabeth.

> At that time Mary got ready and hurried to a town in the
> hill country of Judea, where she entered Zechariah's
> home and greeted Elizabeth. When Elizabeth heard
> Mary's greeting, the baby leaped in her womb, and Eliz-
> abeth was filled with the Holy Spirit. In a loud voice she
> exclaimed: "Blessed are you among women, and blessed
> is the child you will bear! But why am I so favored, that
> the mother of my Lord should come to me? As soon as

the sound of your greeting reached my ears, the baby in my womb leaped for joy. Blessed is she who has believed that the Lord would fulfill his promises to her!"

And Mary said:

"My soul glorifies the Lord

and my spirit rejoices in God my Savior,

for he has been mindful

of the humble state of his servant.

From now on all generations will call me blessed,

for the Mighty One has done great things for
me—

holy is his name.

His mercy extends to those who fear him,

from generation to generation.

He has performed mighty deeds with his arm;

he has scattered those who are proud in their
inmost thoughts.

He has brought down rulers from their thrones

but has lifted up the humble.

He has filled the hungry with good things

but has sent the rich away empty.

He has helped his servant Israel,

remembering to be merciful

to Abraham and his descendants forever,

just as he promised our ancestors."

Mary stayed with Elizabeth for about three months and then returned home.

(Lk 1:39-56)

A scene that could have easily gone awry is a glorious picture of women who embolden women. Mary enters the home of another pregnant woman, and there could have been comparing, jealousy, and passive-aggressiveness. Mary was pregnant with the Messiah, after all, and Elizabeth was not. But instead, Elizabeth flings open the doors, embraces her, welcomes her, identifies with her, and blesses her—"blessed are you among women!" After she is blessed by Elizabeth, Mary is emboldened, propelled, and impelled to proclaim one of the most beautiful prophetic songs in Scripture. Will you be an Elizabeth today?

It brings me a tremendous amount of joy to sit with younger women pursuing ministry. The next generation of leaders give me so much hope for the future of the bride of Christ. We need all capable hands on deck reaching out to the next generation, pulling them to the table, pushing them to pulpits, teaching them the Bible, speaking words of wisdom to them, coming alongside them in leadership, and instilling confidence in them. What we decide to do with the next generation has a ripple effect for our daughters, and their daughters, and their daughters. Who will you, dear sister, embolden today?

AN EMBOLDENED WOMEN'S MINISTRY

Many women who affirm women in leadership are often opposed to women's ministries in churches. For some, women's ministry seems like the church is sequestering gifted women in order to keep them out of the main duties of the church. For some, women's ministry feels a bit watered down and is for women who fit a certain type of mold. Sarah Bessey shares this sentiment in her book, *Jesus Feminist*:

Once I was married, I tried to make the women's ministry thing fit, but most of the time, it was just as ill-fitting as that emerald-green sparkle outfit. First of all, it was hard to get there: I worked full-time, and it seemed that most women's ministry events met on weekdays. But every once in a while I came to the evening events, dutiful and obedient to my responsibilities. We usually sat at round tables of eight, painstakingly decorated, to fill out worksheets. Question time was a staring contest of awkward silences, punctuated with responses suitable for consumption by total strangers thrown together for two hours over tea. Sometimes there were craft nights. But even when I was finally the target demographic of most church ladies' ministries, a stay-at-home mom right in the thick of my life, tired with a never-ending pile of laundry, still I didn't fit.[6]

Traditionally, women's ministries thrive in churches where women are not allowed to teach, preach, and lead because it is the one place (besides children's ministry) where women are able to exercise their gifts of leadership, teaching, and preaching. In fact, it has been my observation that most booming women's ministries in America have been in these types of churches. If a woman isn't allowed to teach, preach, or lead in the larger congregation, of course she's going to make her way into a women's ministry. She's starving to use her gifts! As a result, strong proponents for the *full inclusion* of women in the church tend to buck against women's ministry for the ways it secludes gifted women from the rest of the congregation.

Some of these women contend that women's ministry has been reduced to craft parties, and only works for a certain type of woman. But I believe women's ministry has its place in even the most inclusive churches for women. When women get together to pray, seek justice, study the Bible, and encourage one another, incredible things happen. Furthermore, when a women's ministry isn't seen as an end in itself, but as a conduit to propel women to use their gifts in the local church and in the world, watch out—the church lights up a little bit more.

I propose, then, that churches who have women's Bible ministries become more intentional in empowering women by not only offering video-driven Bible studies, craft parties, and Advent teas, but also allowing them to teach, serve, get their hands dirty, do justice, preach, and lead.

I am certainly not against women's Bible studies where an author leads a study on DVD; studies like this are edifying, encouraging, and God-honoring. But things *can* become unhealthy when women's ministries *only* use a DVD curriculum. When churches use DVD curriculums exclusively for their women's Bible studies and the preaching staff of the church is all male, the women in the church are never given the opportunity to use their gifts in teaching and preaching. Furthermore, the ministry is then centered on some celebrity author-teacher who will never meet with the community in the flesh.

I often wonder how many women in these churches even *know* that they have been given gifts of teaching and exhortation, because they never have the opportunity to use them! When the Bible teacher is local, she is able to respond pastorally to situations and can contextualize her content. So please, give your women commentaries; teach them how to do exegesis, dig deep, and create a Bible study; and let them use their gifts. This is an emboldened women's ministry. I love the way Sarah Bessey describes it:

> I think you have a great women's ministry when the women of your community fall wildly in love with Jesus. Church ladies like this are the overflow of women who are empowered to lead, to challenge, to seek justice and love mercy, to follow Jesus to the ends of the earth like our church mothers and fathers of the past. You have a great women's ministry when there is room for everyone. You have a great women's ministry when you have detoxed from the world's views and unattainable standards for women and begun to celebrate the everyday women of valor, sitting next to you, and when you encourage, affirm, and welcome the diversity of women—their lives, their voices, their experiences—to the community. You have a great women's ministry when your women are ministering—to the world, to the church, to one another—pouring out freely the grace they have received, however God has gifted them, including cooking and crafts, strategy, and leadership.[7]

WHY DOES ANY OF THIS MATTER?

It might seem like I am nitpicking or trying to mess up things that might be working for local congregations. But it *does* matter because even in churches that affirm women in ministry, women can become sidelined; women's spiritual muscles become weak; women find places to use their unique gifts outside of the church; and consequently we underutilize half of the church. And although I know it's not for all women, I believe women's ministry in the local churches is beneficial and edifying. It can be a safe place for women to discover their gifts and gain confidence in what the Spirit of the living God can do in and through them; it can be a place where women soar—all for the edification of the people of God, the mission of God, and the glorification of God.

So let us celebrate women's ministries in churches, but let's celebrate it as one of the many places women can grow in their knowledge of God, the Bible, and theology, and also grow in their gifts. And let it be a place where women celebrate one another's gifts. Let us celebrate and embolden one another, just like Elizabeth did with Mary. Go out of your way for one another, be generous with opportunities for one another, open doors for each other, train, admonish, and encourage one another. This, my dear sisters, is what emboldened women do: we embolden one another.

SIX

MARRIAGE, FAMILY, AND SINGLENESS IN MINISTRY

WE COULDN'T HAVE BEEN MUCH OLDER than eight or nine when the neighborhood kids and I decided to hold a mock wedding in the middle of the woods that began at the end of our street.[1] We didn't want our parents to find out about our wedding, so we figured the woods would keep our secret safe. I got to be the bride, and if my memory recalls correctly, I mostly was interested in the end part: the kiss. Growing up, I was a bit of a "hopeless romantic." I would often adorn my head with a pillow case for a wedding veil and have pretend weddings alone in my bedroom. Disney princess movies were the best because the princess always ended up with prince charming. There's rarely been a time in my life when I *haven't* hoped to be married. Growing up with parents who have loved each other now for over forty-five years, it was difficult for me to imagine my future without marriage—that is, until I began to navigate my new future as a called minister.

I attended Olivet Nazarene University in the early 2000s as a ministry major. One of the common jokes on campus was that the female students only enrolled in school to get their MRS degree. While it may have been a joke, there was certainly some truth to this. Many were engaged by their sophomore year and married by their junior year. Strangely, one of the most common things I heard from some hopeful classmates was an odd comment that went something like this: "I feel *called* to be a pastor's wife, so I am waiting to date a ministry major." I most *certainly* never heard a male student say anything remotely close that! So then, knowing that I was headed toward pastoral ministry, any hopes of marriage began to fade into the background. Who on earth would want to marry a *female* pastor? Clearly that's *weird*. There were times when the only way anyone would ever marry me is if *they too* were a pastor and we'd be able to find a local church to serve together. But even that seemed far-fetched.

When I met Jeff, my husband, we developed a great friendship that eventually turned into a romantic relationship. When things started to get serious, we began having many conversations about what marriage would look like with me being a pastor. Being young and in love, there was hardly anything that could be a deal breaker. We did, of course, talk through countless scenarios of this unique calling, but I don't think either of us ever fully knew what it would look like. And when we got married, I don't think either of us had any idea of the difference between an *egalitarian* marriage and a *complementarian* marriage.[2] Marriage, ministry, and this crazy thing called *submission* have been part of the journey for us. Jeff and I don't have a perfect marriage, by any means, but I am in this for the long haul with him, and he is in it with me.

Our marriage, which isn't very traditional, has always been a little confusing for many on the outside looking in. On two different occasions Jeff has left two significant dream jobs so we could move across the country to serve another church. The first time, Jeff was working for Lockheed Martin as an engineer on the next presidential helicopter, and he moved to take on a glamorous server role at Olive Garden. The second time, Jeff was in a highly classified program as an engineer for Northrop Grumman and then became a stay-at-home dad for four months. Both times *we* took a leap of faith, totally trusting that we were following the Spirit's leading and that something would eventually work out. And something always did, but not without a lot of questions from those on the outside looking in. Here are some of the questions and comments we most often hear:

- Why would a husband ever leave a job for his wife's calling?

- How does the wife submit to the husband when the wife is the pastor?

- Isn't it hard for your wife to always be in the limelight?

- Tara Beth, you'll stay home full-time when you have children, right?

- If your wife is the pastor, then who takes care of the kids?

- Who is in charge at home?

- Tara Beth, if you're at this party, who has the kids?

- Tara Beth, how can you pastor with small children at home?

Among Christians who love perfectly organized gender roles, our marriage causes a lot of confusion because it flips the traditional norm upside down. That is, our marriage doesn't reflect the "traditional" model, which didn't even arise until the nineteenth century, where the husband rules the household and the wife stays home with the kids and is devoted to all things domestic. In this model, the wife always submits to her husband's wishes. But this is more of a *doormat* model, and not a *biblical* model. Our marriage, family, and ministry works because when it comes to gender roles, Jeff and I don't box one another in, we partner together in ways that work best for us. And because of this partnering I am emboldened to teach, preach, and lead. I submit to Jeff, yes, but Jeff also submits to me.

Let's do some digging in Ephesians 5—you know, the controversial submission passage: "Wives, submit yourselves to your own husbands" (Eph 5:22).

It wasn't until Jeff and I were going through marriage counseling that I began to reflect on this passage. By that time I was a driven young woman with dreams of pastoring a church. As we were going through counseling, I was at first angry with this passage. I even told the pastor officiating our wedding that it could not be read during the ceremony. The idea of submitting to Jeff as the only leader in the marriage terrified me. I was theologically trained; Jeff was not. So did that mean I had to follow Jeff's lead with pastoral calling or ministry decisions? Over time, however, Jeff and I began to embrace a fuller understanding of what exactly Paul was getting at in this glorious section of Scripture.

This is one of the more debated and even abused passages in the New Testament. In today's context, the word *submissive* is most often understood as weakness, giving up control, and being dominated by a more privileged party. In other words, this passage is understood to be teaching that the wife is the weaker partner who submits to the more powerful partner, the one at the top of the hierarchy, the husband. In today's Western cultural landscape, the word *submission* alone makes one's skin crawl. But a deeper look will reveal that submission, and even self-denial and sacrifice for the sake of the other, is a distinctly Christian idea and looks a lot like Jesus.

In Paul's letter to the Ephesians, Paul writes about a life characterized by the Spirit. In Ephesians 5:21, Paul urges all Christians to "submit to one another out of reverence for Christ." Note that it does not say some Christians submit to other Christians. In other words, Spirit-filled and Spirit-led Christians are impelled and propelled to submit to one another out of their love for Christ. If anything, the submission that the apostle Paul writes of is one of utter selflessness and sacrifice for the other. We are to have a you-before-me posture before all people.

This theme of submission is not unique to Ephesians 5. It is also found in 1 Corinthians 16:15-16, where Paul urges both male and female believers to submit to other male and female believers in the house of Stephanas. All members of the household would not *exclude* servants and women. Therefore, Paul is asking Christians to submit even to *servants*! Prophets are called to submit to other prophets (1 Cor 14:32); Christians, above all, are called to submit to Christ (Rom 12:3; Gal 5:13). Submission is most often thought of as the husband having control and power over the wife, but Paul notes that women have authority over their husband's body in the same way that men have authority over their wife's body (1 Cor 7:4). Furthermore, when Paul urges all Christians to submit to *one another*, it is impossible for there to be a more powerful or privileged party in view. (Not to mention Galatians 3:28!) Could it be that husbands too should submit to their wives out of love and sacrifice?

Paul goes on:

> Wives, submit yourselves to your own husbands as you do to the Lord. For the husband is the head of the wife as Christ is the head of the church, his body, of which he is the Savior. Now as the church submits to Christ, so also wives should submit to their husbands in everything.
>
> Husbands, love your wives, just as Christ loved the church and gave himself up for her to make her holy, cleansing her by the washing with water through the word, and to present her to himself as a radiant church, without stain or wrinkle or any other blemish, but holy and blameless. In this same way, husbands ought to love their wives as their own bodies. He who loves his wife loves himself. After all, no one ever hated their own body, but they feed and care for their body, just as Christ does the church—for we are members of his body. "For this reason a man will leave his father and mother and be united to his wife, and the two will become one flesh." This is a profound mystery—but I am talking about Christ and the church. However, each one of you also must love

his wife as he loves himself, and the wife must respect her husband. (Eph 5:22-33)

Paul writes this in the context of "a gender and sexual revolution."[3] What McKnight and other scholars call the "new Roman woman" was dominating, aggressive, argumentative, strong-willed, and even provocative.[4] So when Paul writes, "wives submit to your husbands," it is not in an oppressive, top-down hierarchy sort of way, but is instead a radical act of subversive love and selflessness from the wife toward the husband.

Furthermore, as a result of the fall, humanity almost instinctively seeks to hold dominance over one another. Let's be real for a moment. This reality plays out in our marriage often. I confess that I am probably the more stubborn of the two of us, and I confess (with some shame) that Jeff is often the first one to submit or apologize. But in heated moments, we naturally attempt to seek dominance over the other. For us, it usually is over the pettiest things, and I don't recall a time when the two of us couldn't see eye to eye on a big decision. Perhaps it's because in big decisions we recognize the importance of slowing down, being prayerful, and weighing out as many options as possible. But when it comes to how to parent the kids in a particular situation, where to go for dinner, or something not going the way we had hoped, we often struggle to practice mutual submission. Mutual submission, no doubt, takes work, intentionality, sacrifice, and a lot of prayer. Many days it's a daily battle of the will to promote Jeff's self-interest over my own, but it is the way of the cross. It is the way of submission and love. Scot McKnight writes,

The fall turned the woman to seek dominance over the man, and the fall turned the man to seek dominance over the woman. A life of struggling for control is the way of life for the fallen. But the good news story of the Bible is that the fall eventually gives way to new creation; the fallen can be reborn and re-created. Sadly, the church has far too often perpetuated the fall as a permanent condition. Perpetuating the fall entails failing to restore creation conditions when it comes to male and female relationships.[5]

So in just a few sentences, Paul appeals to the new familial order established in Christ: a structure where women are no longer dominated by men but are loved sacrificially, and a structure where men are not dominated by women but are submitted to lovingly. Paul turns the husband and the wife toward the way of the new creation in Christ.

- In Christ, there is not a privileged party in marriage. (Gal 3:28)

- In Christ, husband and wife stand on equal footing.

- In Christ, a husband doesn't serve his own self-interest before his wife's.

- In Christ, the husband and wife work to always put the other first.

- In Christ, a wife doesn't serve her own self-interest before her husband's.

- In Christ, a husband doesn't control his wife with a top-down authority.

- In Christ, a wife doesn't have dominance over her husband.

- In Christ, husbands radically and counterculturally *love their wives just as Christ loved the church and gave himself up for her.*

How does Christ love the church? And how did Christ give himself up for her?

Paul informs us:

Who, being in very nature God,
 did not consider equality with God something to be
  used to his own advantage;
rather, he made himself nothing
 by taking the very nature of a servant,
 being made in human likeness.
And being found in appearance as a man,
 he humbled himself
 by becoming obedient to death—
  even death on a cross!
Therefore God exalted him to the highest place
 and gave him the name that is above every name,
that at the name of Jesus every knee should bow,
 in heaven and on earth and under the earth,
and every tongue acknowledge that Jesus Christ is Lord,
 to the glory of God the Father. (Phil 2:6-11)

Did you catch that? *He took on the very nature of a servant. He humbled himself by becoming obedient to death.* Love, then, sounds a lot like *submission.* Furthermore, in Ephesians 5:21 we are reminded that both the husband and wife submit to Christ; therefore, all authority and power belongs to the One who reigns eternally—King Jesus, the one who gave it all so selflessly and sacrificially. Control has already been surrendered to

Christ; the husband and wife, then, have mutually given up control to King Jesus. Both *submission* and *love* are based on the couple's relation to Christ.

Paul paints a picture of marital relations as *the way of Jesus*: humility, love, sacrifice, and unity. It's husband and wife hand in hand, knee to knee, trying to out serve one another. "You first!" says the husband. "No, you first!" says the wife. As the husband and the wife both submit to Christ, radical acts of love, selflessness, and sacrifice flow toward one another; it is the central ingredient to the Spirit-led life. In the very same way that Jesus redefines greatness as a servant, so it is in mutual submission: "whoever wishes to be great among you must be your servant, and whoever wishes to be first among you must be your slave" (Mt 20:26-27 NRSV). Mutual submission looks a lot like Jesus. Because of mutual submission, Jeff emboldens me to the serve the church. He doesn't embolden me to serve the church because I am obeying his orders, but because of the daily, loving sacrifice he makes. Jeff is a proud pastor's husband, and he does it out of fear and reverence for Christ.

Carla Sunberg has been married to her husband, Chuck, for thirty-four years. The Sunbergs are pastors and missionaries, and Carla now serves as a general superintendent in the Church of the Nazarene. At this season in their lives, Carla is in the limelight, so to speak. She is in high demand for speaking engagements, and she is often seated at the table.

I recall one time hearing her preach as her husband adoringly watched her from the front row. As I watched him watch her, it was as though he were a seventeen-year-old boy newly smitten with a girl. I later saw them walking the beach hand in hand, and I could tell they were happy to be in one another's presence. I later asked her, "How has it worked for thirty-four years?" Her answer was simple but profound. "It's been a journey of give-and-take. Sometimes I have to take the backseat in our ministry journey, and other times he takes the backseat, but we always do it together. We always have to ask ourselves what's most important during that season. But no matter what season we are in, we make time for our marriage." Chuck and Carla Sunberg so beautifully portray a marriage emboldened by the Spirit to do the work of the kingdom.

THE PASTOR'S HUSBAND

I am certain it's not an easy task, and there are no books out there on how to be a pastor's husband—literally. Jeff is a trailblazer, but you wouldn't know it by his posture. The following are a few thoughts from Jeff on what it means to be a pastor's husband:

> In the years before I met Tara Beth, I never formalized in my mind what it would look like to be married. Sure, I had disparate thoughts and ideas, but never really a cohesive picture. Maybe that worked out to my advantage, because it most certainly would not have been the spouse of a senior pastor. While it's true that many of the situations and issues we face are unique to swapped gender roles, many are not.
>
> It should be of no surprise then that one way to embolden Tara Beth is to keep her balanced. Many pastors struggle with balancing time for family regardless of

gender. I think that is something important to remember;
the burden of the call for women can tug just as strong as
for any man. That is why we talk about opportunities and
obligations, and consider the impact on the family. Sometimes the way we maintain balance results in slightly crazy
plans of carting around the boys for military-timed
meetings with Mommy as she goes from one meeting to
another, but it's worth it. It could be easy to become re-
sentful and wish my wife just had a normal job or stayed at
home, but I think then that would be failing on two fronts.
You see, I don't view the ways I help Tara as simply a spouse
supporting the career and aspirations of their partner.
Rather, I see it also as living out my identity as a Christian.

I think most people who know Tara Beth would agree
that she has a calling on her life for full-time ministry. It
is sensible then to view my support of Tara as supporting
her ministry, but I believe it really is more than that. As
her spouse, we are connected—one, in fact—and it would
be impractical to think that a calling would only be one-
sided. Sure, we have different gifts and edify the body in
different ways, but my actions and how I live out my relationship with Tara Beth can greatly impact her ability to
impact the kingdom to her fullest. Therefore, emboldening Tara is really no more than being obedient, and although our day-to-day might look a little different than
many in the church, that's the life we've been called to live.

But just because we are called does not mean all the
answers have been given or all the pitfalls are known.
We're still learning and growing on this adventure together,

and who knows, maybe someday we can finally attend a conference together and not have everyone ask what church I'm pastoring (as Tara Beth stands off to the side).

Jeff is another guy in the body of Christ who deeply loves Jesus, deeply loves the church, and deeply loves his wife. At this stage in our lives—with little ones at home—Jeff's most profound ministry is simply showing up. With my busy schedule, full of demands and evening commitments, Jeff isn't able to lead or start a new ministry in the church, and I don't know if that is necessarily his cup of tea. When we didn't have little ones at home, Jeff's ministry was often behind the tech deck, behind a camera, or behind a computer. Jeff is present— present to me, present to the congregation, and present to God. On Sunday mornings Jeff is right in the front row, right next to me, and prayerfully watching me preach. Every Saturday night I read through my sermon with Jeff, and he listens with a calming and prayerful presence, and then often offers helpful feedback. When I have a week full of evening commitments, Jeff is prayerfully and lovingly doing what he loves—being Dad. Jeff's deep love for Jesus, for the church, and for me isn't manifested in the limelight, but he shows his love and support by his simple and supportive presence. He's always there, always encouraging, always supporting, always serving, always loving, and always present. I am reminded of Joseph's quiet presence to God and to Mary in the first Advent:

> This is how the birth of Jesus the Messiah came about: His mother Mary was pledged to be married to Joseph, but before they came together, she was found to be pregnant

through the Holy Spirit. Because Joseph her husband was faithful to the law, and yet did not want to expose her to public disgrace, he had in mind to divorce her quietly.

But after he had considered this, an angel of the Lord appeared to him in a dream and said, "Joseph son of David, do not be afraid to take Mary home as your wife, because what is conceived in her is from the Holy Spirit. She will give birth to a son, and you are to give him the name Jesus, because he will save his people from their sins."

All this took place to fulfill what the Lord had said through the prophet: "The virgin will conceive and give birth to a son, and they will call him Immanuel" (which means "God with us").

When Joseph woke up, he did what the angel of the Lord had commanded him and took Mary home as his wife. But he did not consummate their marriage until she gave birth to a son. And he gave him the name Jesus. (Mt 1:18-25)

There isn't a lot said about Joseph, but the picture we do get is of a man of faithful and quiet presence in the middle of a terribly inconvenient interruption. But he never calls it an interruption or an inconvenience; instead, Joseph shows us the way of sacrifice, service, and selfless love. During the first Christmas, Mary is in the spotlight, and while Joseph's role is critical at this time, it's in a quiet, faithful-presence sort of way. Joseph is there. Joseph shows up. Joseph obeys God. Joseph loves Mary.

I often wonder and even have asked Jeff if this is what he imagined his future would be like. Jeff always says he never dreamed he'd be a pastor's "wife"—he jokes—but he says he wouldn't want it any other way. Did he imagine a stay-at-home wife and mom who was good at cooking and all things domestic instead of this? If so, by Jeff's ministry of presence, we would never know it. Through Jeff's ministry of showing up, obedience to God, and love to the church and myself, he is instrumental to God's mission in this world. Just as Joseph laid down his life, his goals, his hopes, and his dreams for the mission of God, I see the same in Jeff. Together, we are a team, and I can't imagine ministry without him.

It's difficult to be a married woman in ministry without a husband who supports, encourages, and emboldens. So listen closely, dear husbands. If the Spirit is doing something unique in your wife, you have the chance to be part of reclaiming the kingdom imagination for your wife. Imagine the lives that are waiting to be changed because of your wife's gifts. Imagine her kingdom impact. Your wife's calling isn't just *her calling*, dear husband—it's *your calling* too. So get on your knees, pray for her, pray for wisdom, pray for guidance. Look to Jesus and see how he laid down his life; lay down your life for her, serve her, love her, cherish her, encourage her, push her, and *embolden her*. What are you willing to give up, set aside, or do for the sake of God's mission? Dear husbands, what is your plan to embolden your wife today?

LETTING GO OF DOING IT ALL

On a regular basis I hear, "How do you do it all, Tara Beth?" Well, I don't. I have a journey partner, though it has taken me years to figure that out. Perhaps if you are a female in leadership, you've heard it too. When our first child, Caleb Daniel Leach, was born, our world was totally rocked. As a young pastor, a full-time seminarian, and now a mama living in a wealthy suburban community where most mamas stayed home, I was quickly pulled into the deep oblivion called "mom guilt." Caleb was born right about the time the Pinterest craze and mommy blogs were captivating the imaginations of mommies all over the nation. I would spend hours reading mom blogs and scrolling through Pinterest and I, like many others, began collecting blogs, images, and ideas on how to be the perfect mom. At the same time, I believed I needed to have straight As in school, a perfectly clean house, perfectly crafted home-cooked meals, and a perfectly fit body. I wanted, truly wanted, to have and do it all. But I never could—that was a myth. Sheryl Sandberg notes,

> Each of us makes choices constantly between work and family, exercising and relaxing, making time for others and taking time for ourselves. Being a parent means making adjustments, compromises, and sacrifices every day. For most people, sacrifices and hardships are not a choice, but a necessity.[6]

It all came to a head when I was in my third year of seminary and my boys were one and three. I was preaching sometimes one or two sermons a week, and I was also a teaching assistant for Scot McKnight. Life was so very good, but things on the home front were not—that is, that's what I told myself. I came home one night after a long night of class and ministry. Jeff already had the boys tucked into bed. When I walked into our bedroom, I saw a mountain of laundry on top of our bed. I'd like to say that this was a rare sighting; however, it was a regular occurrence during those days. You see, Jeff and I were good about washing clothes, but we were terrible with putting them away. Usually the only time we were able to put laundry away was very late at night when we were both already exhausted from a full day of work and parenting. That night the laundry pile was larger than usual. (It could have been named as a landmark it was so big.) But I was too exhausted to do anything about it, so I slid under the covers and mountain of laundry and attempted to go to sleep. However, after lying in bed for about thirty minutes, I became incredibly hot underneath the mountain. Agitated from the heat, but too exhausted to put the laundry away, I laid there with thoughts of failure swirling in my mind:

- You're a failure.

- If you were a good mom and a good wife, you would have had all of these clothes put away.

- Your house is always a mess. You should be ashamed.

- You could have done better on your paper.

- You are fat. How will you ever get that baby weight off?

- Your children have had McDonald's twice this week. All the other moms do organic, home-cooked meals every night.

- Noah's first birthday is in three weeks. You have nothing planned. You're a bad mom.

I laid there underneath the massive pile of laundry as these thoughts of failure swirled in my brain. I was not only feeling like a failure but was also angry and jealous. I was angry and jealous that all of the other pastors on staff had a stay-at-home spouse to help with all of the duties at home so they could focus on ministry while at church and on family while home. I always heard about these so called stay-at-home spouses and would often say to myself, *I want one of those!* I would often daydream about what it must be like to come home to a clean house, happy kids, and a warm meal after a long day of ministry. On the other hand, I was angry and jealous of all of my girlfriends who would walk into Starbucks at 10 a.m. with yoga pants on, hair on top of their head, and sweat on their brows as they had just finished their morning workout, while I was already several hours into writing a sermon. These same moms would sit around tables with a coffee in their hand and gab and laugh with their girlfriends all morning. It was a constant game of comparison. Sheryl Sandberg shares a similar struggle:

> Like me, most of the women I know do a great job of worrying that we don't measure up. We compare our efforts at work to those of our colleagues, usually men, who typically have far fewer responsibilities at home. Then we compare our efforts at home to those of mothers who dedicate themselves solely to their families.[7]

So there I was, simmering in anger, jealousy, and heat from the pile of clothes. I turned to elbow my sweet, sweet husband, who was soundly asleep next to me. *I shouldn't have to lie here alone in my own misery. He needed to suffer with me, after all!* I woke Jeff with a sharp jab of the elbow; his big, blue eyes stared at me with a confused look.

"Jeff! Why don't you ever help me? I'm a failure in everything, and I am completely drowning." After a few slow blinks Jeff responded groggily, "What are you talking about, babe?" You see, rarely was Jeff bothered by the things that bothered me. It wasn't that he didn't care, and it wasn't that he didn't want to help, and it wasn't that he wasn't involved; he just didn't see things the same as I saw them. Jeff has always been mister stress-free, happy-go-lucky Jeff. So that night as I unloaded all my frustrations of our current "failures," Jeff calmly said, "Babe, why didn't you tell me these things were bothering you?" Jeff had no idea that I was drowning under the weight of thinking I had to do it all. And then it dawned on me; I never once asked for his help. I never once tried to delegate responsibilities in the home, for organizing birthday parties, or for cooking dinner. I totally bought into the myth that I had to do it all, and when I failed, I placed blame on Jeff, my biggest cheerleader and partner in life, family, and ministry.

Ever since that day, underneath the pile of laundry and a pile of worry, Jeff and I have together been undoing any narrative that claims that *I need to do it and have it all*. Especially now as a senior pastor, I have let go of that story. Jeff and I *don't* buy into the false narrative that says women are bad moms for working. Jeff and I *don't* buy into the false narrative that says women should only stay home and not work when children are at home. Jeff and I *don't* buy into the false narrative that declares perfect balance is achievable. Jeff and I *do* believe that our lives are totally wrapped up in following King Jesus, serving his bride, and joining him on mission in this world. That means life sometimes gets cluttered, and laundry sometimes piles up, schedules can be complicated and unpredictable, and some weeks we are out of balance. But Jeff and I are in this crazy parenting and mission thing together, and we wouldn't have it any other way.

THE EMBOLDENED SINGLE WOMAN

Being married is in no way a prerequisite for ministry. I have plenty of girlfriends who lead out of their singleness, and it is a beautiful thing. A fellow pastor was recently going through credentialing interviews for her denomination. After her interview, she walked away completely disheartened that normal interview questions on theology, spiritual gifts, and basic testimony were never discussed. Instead, the interviewers wanted to talk all about her relational status—she is single. "How will you minister as a single woman?" "What happens if you marry someone who doesn't support you?" She said she felt like her marital status was more important than her calling, gifts, and testimony.

Interestingly, although the apostle Paul admonished all who are single to stay single so they would not be distracted, unmarried ministers in the North American context are all too often marginalized. Churches and Christian organizations that think it's better to hire married ministers are sadly selling themselves short. In a *Christianity Today* article, Lore Ferguson contends that singles have an advantage in ministry. She notes:

1. Godly singles will be more available for ministry and study than their married counterparts.

2. Walking unpartnered equips singles to deal with painful realities of life without seeking solace in a spouse.

3. If Christ asks for holiness, purity, and chastity from the unmarried, then we need models of those who are living out those virtues in prolonged seasons.

She then implores churches to pay attention:

> Being content in Christ while single is not as simple as three points and a poem. Sometimes it is a very real war against flesh. The church desperately needs single pastors and ministers who understand that prolonged warring. They understand the agony of having not yet arrived to eternity's shores in a deep and daily way.
>
> Church, fill your staff with single men and women. Pursue them for ministry places. Do not always make the comfortable choice of a potential staffer who has 2.5 kids and a house in the suburbs.[8]

In the 1800s, people of color—let alone women of color—were rarely welcomed to places of visible ministry. Amanda Berry Smith had much going against her. She was a widow. She was a former slave. She was an African American. But she was an emboldened woman. Although there were seemingly more barriers than open doors, Amanda kept her eyes resolutely on King Jesus. Amanda pushed through her barriers and declared, "I was not so well known then and many people were shy of me, and are yet. But, I belong to Royalty and am well acquainted with the King of Kings and am better known and better understood among the great family above than I am on earth."[9] Amanda saw who she was as a daughter of the King, not as a forgotten daughter in the empire.

Amanda was no stranger to taunting and humiliation, but she had a kingdom vision and was a woman on a mission. She didn't have a husband to listen to her sermons the night before she'd stand before hundreds of people; she didn't have a husband to comfort her when she was humiliated or shamed for her color and gender; but she did have the Spirit of the living God. Amanda led with power, boldness, and courage. She traveled all over the globe to preach the message she was so passionate about: King Jesus.

Early on at PazNaz, I met an emboldened woman who was a long-time missionary in Bolivia and had recently returned to the mission field after many years back in her home country. Sharon and I have had many coffee conversations about Jesus, mission, formational practices, and the Spirit. Sharon is an emboldened single woman who shares her journey of singleness and life on mission:

> Since childhood God has uniquely led me on a journey to embrace my singleness as a choice and calling. I see this as a privilege that has freed me to focus my time and energy using my ministry gifts. During my sixteen years as a missionary in Bolivia I have had my share of struggles and successes working through different leadership ministry roles. I see myself acting creatively, somewhat like a chameleon. My gifts and ministry were sometimes hidden or camouflaged behind the scenes, but the Holy Spirit has helped me discern when to quickly and colorfully reappear and forge ahead effectively into new ministry opportunities.
>
> As Christ has led me to venture into ministry and leadership, there have been victories and breakthroughs

while battling an environment of questions and confrontations related to my gender. But I continue to be motivated and inspired by the female leaders in the Bible, single missionary biographies, and female evangelists and preachers today who courageously have stepped out in faith to be obedient to Christ's leading. They do so bravely amidst opposition and some being restored to ministry after significant setbacks.

During my Christian life I have felt God nurturing a strong sense of personal identity. Being led by the Spirit has meant growing in obedience and self-denial, and humbly surrendering to Christ's will. Not always practiced, but this is my ideal. As a single I have a strong desire for a spiritual covering and spiritual accountability. Being in relationship and under the authority of the bride of Christ (church) also alleviates the need I have for a sense of belonging.

Resigning from the mission field in 1998 was the hardest thing I have ever done. I was crushed. I tried to cope as best I could and have lived through some desert years. I must confess to sometimes just living a "normal Christian routine," trying to justify this as OK when in reality I was hiding spiritual complacency.

In the last few years I have done a lot of soul searching and tried to take responsibility for my own spiritual growth by practicing spiritual disciplines. I continue to grow and listen to the Holy Spirit. There is a lot more joy in my life as I am experiencing the presence of Jesus.

I am very thankful for godly pastoral staff at PazNaz, preaching series, Sermon on the Mount Bible study, and encouragement from pastors. Above all, I am indebted to and grateful for God's love and faithfulness, to rebirth in me a spiritual hunger and thirst, for creating in me a new heart to live out the mission.

Emboldened women aren't empowered because of their age, gender, marital status, or parenting status, but because of Spirit-filled and courageous colaborers in Christ who open doors for, include, and come alongside of their sisters. Emboldened women are empowered by spouses, children, friends, churches, and the Spirit of the living God. Lead from where you are, dear sisters. Lead from where you are, in the power of the Spirit. Do it with courage, gusto, and boldness.

PART 2

A VISION FOR AN EM**BOLD**ENED CHURCH

SEVEN

AN EMBOLDENED MISSION

"DON'T YOU JUST WANT TO PROVE them all wrong and win this fight, Tara Beth?" asked my girlfriend as we sat across from one another at a local pizza joint. I hesitated for a moment, and then quickly blurted out, "No. No, I don't. I mean, yes, at times I do, but ultimately no." Don't get me wrong. I have had plenty of moments of daydreaming when I imagine running into an outspoken complementarian in heaven and saying, "See! I told you so! Do you see how many women you've sidelined in the church?" I have imagined such things, but I also know that deep down this is not the reason I desire to see women living into their full potential in the kingdom. Truth is, I'm mad about mission and edification for the people of God, and I believe that if women make this battle about winning this fight for the sake of winning this fight, we will lose sight of the wondrous mission that we have been invited into.

It's about *mission*. And as long as women are held back in the church, I believe the church will continue to miss out on the fullness of mission we have been invited to participate in. While I care about equal rights and justice, I also care deeply about the mission of God—which includes justice, equality, and inclusion—and if the church's participation in the mission of God is limited because women are sidelined, then I am incredibly interested in seeing men *and* women *emboldened* to participate in the mission of God in this world.

WHY IT'S NOT MERELY JUSTICE

Justice in the Western ideological context is based on human rights and equality. Justice is important for order, fairness, and to create a certain kind of society. Justice conforms a society in order to protect, maintain fairness and equality, and keep order. Human rights and equality influence constructs and institutions in an effort to achieve justice in every level of society. Justice, no doubt, is a theme that rolls throughout the Bible's big story. While justice is important, this is not why I am so passionate about seeing women live into their full potential in the body of Christ. We can't stop at justice. It isn't about *my rights*; it isn't about *fairness*.

One day when I picked up my boys from school, my preschooler, Noah, walked out with an adorable little white pumpkin. He was so proud of the pumpkin he even declared that he was going to sleep with it. His older brother, Caleb, was green with envy. He stared at the pumpkin as we drove away from the school on that beautiful California afternoon. Elephant tears rolled down his face as he erupted, "Not fair! It's really not fair, I should get a pumpkin too!" Feeling desperate, I assured him that he too would get a pumpkin. He then said, "An orange one?" To which I said, "Of course, honey, you can have an orange one!" You won't be surprised by his younger brother's reaction when he said, "But that's not fair! Mine is white, I want an orange one too!" Fairness, you see, is a little like that. Fairness and justice are happy and settled when everyone gets what is deserved. But justice and fairness have an earlier finish line than mission. The goal is complete and achieved as soon as everyone has equal pumpkins. And what if everyone isn't supposed to have orange pumpkins? What if some are to have white pumpkins or yellow pumpkins?

If the single goal were about justice, then our focus can be too easily reduced to pushing an equal number of men and women to the pulpit without any sort of testing and approving. Let's face it, not everyone should be teaching, preaching, or leading. This is not an *elitist* thing; it's a *gifting* thing. Some are called to teach; some are called to use their gifts of hospitality. Sometimes people end up behind a pulpit who probably shouldn't be there. But just because someone shouldn't be behind a pulpit doesn't mean they shouldn't be leading. Or just because someone shouldn't be leading doesn't mean they shouldn't be teaching. The beauty of this glorious mission is that God has blessed the bride of Christ with a rainbow of colors and gifts, and the goal isn't for everyone to get a place on the rainbow; rather, the goal is for the colors to shine fully so the world might take notice and see the bright, beautiful, and glorious light shining. The world will see the reflection of Christ as men and women labor together.

When it's only a justice issue, a woman in the pulpit says, "We've won." But when it's a mission issue, a woman in the pulpit says, "We've begun." When it's only a justice issue, the finish line is when everyone has a chance to enter the pulpit, and the path to get there is everyone arguing about whether women should teach, preach, and lead. When it's a mission issue, the finish line is Revelation 21; when Christ returns, the new heaven and the new earth will come together, and the path to get there is men and women serving alongside one another by participating in the redemption of all of creation. The path to get there is not finger pointing, name calling, fighting, and arguing. No, something much bigger is at stake here. The path to get there is the proclamation of King Jesus, standing at the bedside of the weary, breaking bread with our neighbors, feeding the hungry, shepherding churches, teaching Bible studies, and laying hands on the broken. This mission is a big deal, and it's time to get on with it. It isn't merely a justice issue, it's a mission issue—and the mission will continue to be held back without women.

MISSION IS THE HEARTBEAT OF THE CHURCH

In the book of Acts—the beautiful narrative of Pentecost and the formation and mission of the early church—we see an exciting narrative filled with newness, freshness, power, and miracles. Throughout the story we hear the constant proclamation of the life, fulfillment, death, resurrection, and ascension of King Jesus, and the giving of the Holy Spirit. King Jesus and the empowering presence of the Spirit brought together the new people of God and offered salvation, freedom, inclusion, and transformation. The early church was obsessed with the mission of God in Christ. They were mad about living and sharing the mission. Every conversation, every story, and every miracle was connected to mission.

Gordon Fee often reminds readers that the Holy Spirit was an "experienced reality" for the early church. When the Holy Spirit fell afresh on the people of God, we notice an instant change among them. Individuals and the community were transformed; they were empowered and emboldened for mission. One of the most notable changes was in the life of Peter. Peter, one of the twelve disciples in the Gospels, at times seemed not to grasp the fullness of what Jesus was doing. In Mark 8, we see Peter getting it right and wrong in the same moment. It's as if he almost understood the mission of God in Christ. But after confessing that Jesus was the Messiah (v. 29), Peter gets it wrong:

> [Jesus] then began to teach them that the Son of Man must suffer many things and be rejected by the elders, the chief priests and the teachers of the law, and that he must be killed and after three days rise again. He spoke plainly about this, and Peter took him aside and began to rebuke him.
>
> But when Jesus turned and looked at his disciples, he rebuked Peter. "Get behind me, Satan!" he said. "You do not have in mind the concerns of God, but merely human concerns." (Mk 8:31-33)

Poor Peter. He wanted to understand what the mission was all about, but just as quickly as he showed insight into it, he got it wrong. Although we can't blame him for not always catching on (because of his limited knowledge), something supernatural happens to him in Acts 2. Almost immediately after the Holy Spirit fell upon the community, Peter preached with such boldness, conviction, and clarity that it is obvious he had some sort of help. Here's a glimpse of his sermon:

> Then Peter stood up with the Eleven, raised his voice and addressed the crowd: "Fellow Jews and all of you who live in Jerusalem, let me explain this to you; listen carefully to what I say. These people are not drunk, as you suppose. It's only nine in the morning! No, this is what was spoken by the prophet Joel:
>
>> "'In the last days, God says,
>>   I will pour out my Spirit on all people.
>> Your sons and daughters will prophesy,
>>   your young men will see visions,
>>   your old men will dream dreams.
>> Even on my servants, both men and women,
>>   I will pour out my Spirit in those days,
>>   and they will prophesy.
>> I will show wonders in the heavens above
>>   and signs on the earth below,
>>   blood and fire and billows of smoke.
>> The sun will be turned to darkness
>>   and the moon to blood
>>   before the coming of the great and glorious day of
>>   the Lord.
>> And everyone who calls
>>   on the name of the Lord will be saved.'"
>>   (Acts 2:14-21)

In this sermon alone, we can see that at last he finally understood what he had difficulty comprehending before Pentecost.

Peter was supernaturally empowered and emboldened for mission, and he was not only empowered for mission but obsessed with it.

EMPOWERED FOR MISSION

Peter was transformed and empowered, and the early church was transformed and empowered. But they weren't empowered simply for the sake of their gifts being displayed. Peter was transformed and empowered for the sake of *God's mission*. Immediately after Peter's sermon he began preaching, teaching, and proclaiming the life, death, resurrection, and ascension of King Jesus. Peter is so obsessed with mission that he risks his life for it, and he does it with a single-minded focus on Jesus (Acts 3:1-10).

We've been invited into one glorious mission for all of God's people. Christopher Wright says,

> Mission, while it inescapably involves us in planning and action, is not primarily a matter of our activity or our initiative. Mission, from the point of view of our human endeavor, means the committed participation of God's people in the purposes of God for the redemption of the whole creation. Mission is God's. The marvel is that God invites us to join in.[1]

It is indeed a marvel that we are invited to join this mission. If mission means we, the people of God, are committed to participate in the redemption of all of creation, we will live toward and pursue those who are far from Jesus:

- the captive
- the prisoner
- the poor
- the undocumented

- the broken
- the uninsured
- the sick
- the orphan
- the blind
- the widow
- the outcast
- the refugee
- the unemployed
- the incarcerated
- the child with special needs
- the terminally ill
- the marginalized
- the distracted
- the broken hearted
- the lame

When we pursue them and are with them, we point to King Jesus who is

- the Way
- the Truth
- the Life
- the Healer
- the Prince of Peace
- the Redeemer
- the Restorer
- the Vine
- the Lamb who is slain
- the Forgiver of all sins
- Emmanuel
- Author of eternal salvation
- Bread of life
- Bridegroom
- Bright and Morning Star
- Almighty God
- Alpha and Omega
- Anointed One
- Chosen One
- Christ the Lamb
- Comforter
- Creator of all things
- Deliverer
- Eternal
- the Word
- Light of the world
- the Revelation of God
- Resurrection and Life
- our Rock
- our Salvation

And when we point to King Jesus, who is these things, others discover that he offers

- forgiveness of sin
- the gift of the Holy Spirit
- a new heart
- a new family
- a new life
- resurrection
- eternal life
- righteousness
- holiness

- community
- purpose
- grace
- love
- freedom
- restoration
- healing
- identification
- belonging

When I read these lists, I get teary-eyed. Maybe it's the evangelist in me, or maybe it's because I was one who discovered the King when I was sixteen years old, or maybe it's because I've seen the King radically transform lives, or maybe it's all of the above. Regardless, I am in awe that I actually get to be part of this mission. *I get to do this!* It truly is, as Christopher Wright says, "a marvel that God invites us to join in." And I can say firsthand that there is no greater treasure in this life than to sit with someone in these moments of discovery. There are few greater joys than to kneel with someone at the altar as they make life-changing and life-transforming decisions and commitments to Christ. *We get to do this!*

And it matters that we get to do this. When I was a newlywed living in upstate New York, I went on an evening walk with my black Labrador, Maddie. We lived near the Catskills in the Finger Lakes Region, so the landscape was an artist's dream.

Our home was nestled on the edge of luscious green foothills that rolled throughout the region. On that evening, I passed a stone home that looked like it could have come straight from a Thomas Kinkade painting. The smoke from the chimney was billowing up into the crisp, autumn sky. The sun was just beginning to call it a day, with orange, yellow, gold, and indigo dancing in its path. The moment was magical. But it wasn't the sparkling sunset that caught my eye that night. As I passed the home I heard a commotion inside. There were conversations, clanging of glasses, and children laughing. The lights in the home were bursting out of the windows with a warm, yellow glow. I knew that it wouldn't be proper for me to peer in. But I had to take a peek. When I stopped for a moment to look inside, I saw a large family gathered around a table. I could tell they loved each other. I could tell they were unified. I could tell they enjoyed one another. As I looked inside that day, I was overcome by love, joy, and warmth, and I whispered under my breath, "That is exactly the type of family that I want to have someday." It was attractive to me. It pulled me in. I noticed the beauty and joy of the fellowship. *I wanted to be there.*

That's what happens. The people of God on mission is not a place of disunity, a place of gossip, conflict, rejection, pain, strife, and hatred. It is a place where the Spirit's fruits are present in abundance, so much so that the world around the Christian community can't help but *take notice*. It is a community so unified, so beautiful that it stops others in their tracks. Those on the outside can't help but peer in and watch with awe and wonder, and notice the unity, love, warmth, and joy. It is a place of men *and* women at the table, sharing hospitality, sharing gifts, and laying down their lives for each other. It is a place of generosity and care, a place of proclamation and light. And when we get it right, the world sees. When we get it right, the world takes notice. When we get it right, the light *shines bright*. When we get it right, the world *sees Jesus*. When we get it right, *the lost are found, the blind see, the lame walk, the dead live*. This, my friends, is why we gather at the table. Not just so we can have a seat and consume, but so we can have a seat and shine before the world.

IT'S MISSION CRITICAL

In 2017, *Christianity Today* published a story on women missionaries with Wycliffe Bible Translators.[2] The article notes that although in the 1930s and 1940s there was hesitancy to send female missionaries globally, Wycliffe Bible Translators went against the norm. In particular, Wycliffe had been a place where unmarried women had been able to bring their Bible translation skills to the table. The article notes,

> "If it hadn't been for single women over the 70-year history of Wycliffe, half of the translations wouldn't have been completed," according to chief operations officer Russ Hersman.
>
> That legacy has positioned female translators to accelerate today's global translation efforts, address the literacy gap, and empower Christian women in oral-dominated cultures.[3]

Today, women make up 85 percent of the translation force with Wycliffe. Without women, I wonder where Wycliffe would be today. In the 1930s, while many were arguing over whether women could be missionaries, Wycliffe believed it was mission critical to commission their sisters. Today, while many are arguing over male headship, it's mission critical the church gets it right and commissions women to join God in the most glorious and critical mission of all.

WHEN IT'S A MISSION ISSUE, WE PRESS ON

In Luke 10, we get a glimpse of the commissioning of the disciples. In a way, it is their first run at intentional mission. As Jesus commissioned them, he warned them that the mission would indeed be difficult.

> The Lord appointed seventy-two others and sent them two by two ahead of him to every town and place where he was about to go. He told them, "The harvest is plentiful, but the workers are few. Ask the Lord of the harvest, therefore, to send out workers into his harvest field. Go! I am sending you out like lambs among wolves. Do not take a purse or bag or sandals; and do not greet anyone on the road.
>
> "When you enter a house, first say, 'Peace to this house.' If someone who promotes peace is there, your peace will rest on them; if not, it will return to you. Stay there, eating and drinking whatever they give you, for the worker deserves his wages. Do not move around from house to house.
>
> "When you enter a town and are welcomed, eat what is offered to you. Heal the sick who are there and tell them, 'The kingdom of God has come near to you.' But when you enter a town and are not welcomed, go into its streets

and say, 'Even the dust of your town we wipe from our feet as a warning to you. Yet be sure of this: The kingdom of God has come near.' I tell you, it will be more bearable on that day for Sodom than for that town. (Lk 10:1-12)

The mission wasn't going to be easy. It was so tough that Jesus compared it to sheep being sent out to wolves! On any given hard day of ministry, this is a sobering reminder. Mission was never promised to be easy. But we see the disciples and then the apostles participate in this mission anyway! Why? Because much was at stake. Why else? Because Christ compelled them, and they chose obedience over safety. They counted the cost. Being on mission meant persecution, poverty, and martyrdom, and this is played out to the fullest in the book of Acts. But the disciples knew they were not only standing in a grand and glorious narrative, but were also moving toward the redemption of the world. Their loyalties were to King Jesus, even if it meant betraying their deepest loyalties to home and family; their trust and reliance were in God and God's future promises.

Not only was the call costly but there was no time to waste. Jesus was clear: "Do not take a purse or bag or sandals; and do not greet anyone on the road" (v. 4). In other words, *get on with the mission!* Why? *Because the kingdom of God is at hand and we have work to do.*

Some folks will reject the message of Jesus from the mouth of a woman. But mission is at stake. There are other ears to hear the name of Jesus. There are lives to be transformed. Therefore, we don't have time for animosity, to fight fights and harbor bitterness. Mission, you see, compels us to keep on.

Not only do we get to do this, but we *must do this*. So much is at stake, my dear sisters. While God doesn't necessarily need us, he calls us anyway. He beckons the entire bride to jump *all in* and *all out*, even when it's hard. Monica Hardy, pastor of Love, Peace and Joy International Deliverance Ministry in Jacksonville, Florida, knows a thing or two about enduring hardship for the sake of mission. After receiving a doctorate and working in a senior-level position in a local hospital, she had it all. She was a college professor, educated, and a business owner. But friends continued to speak boldly into her life about her leadership in the body of Christ. She took a leap of faith, became an ordained minister, and began teaching and preaching. But the path wasn't easy: "I faced a different set of challenges simply because I was a woman, young and even well educated. I've been told I could not go into the pulpit, I've been told to cover my head or get out of the pulpit, and I've been excluded because I was unmarried."[4]

Dr. Hardy knew, however, that something was at stake if she didn't continue on this mission before her. She knew there was teaching, preaching, and leading to do, so she kept on anyway. She didn't keep on so she could prove to the world that women belonged in the pulpit, but she kept on because the mission of God needed to continue:

> *I can truly say God is GREAT and worthy to be praised. Despite the drastic changes and* challenges in my life, God is truly a provider. When he calls you He is prepared to take care of you. I pastor full time, God has taken the business

I started to another level, and I am engaged to marry another pastor. I've had the opportunity to visit and preach in various churches throughout Florida, and in other states, and in Uganda, Africa; I've had a cable spotlight ministering the word on TV, and I'm on YouTube ministering the word. I've started writing three of five books that God placed in my spirit and asked to assist other pastors with their publications. My fiancé and I are joining churches and doors are opening for greater works! . . .

I truly love and fear God—*it is my goal to please him.* But one of the biggest lessons I have learned is that you cannot fail God; he's all knowing. . . . I have learned that at times it is a lonely walk. Just because people have titles, God is still working on their character, so you will experience hurt on this journey. I have learned people will come and go, *but you must stay focused. I have become bolder and have learned that I must SPEND TIME with God and truly TRUST him at all times.*[5]

Dr. Hardy experienced hardships and trials, but she has kept on and stayed focused because at the end of the day there is a mission to do, and it is her goal to please God.

So no, I don't want to prove to the outspoken complementarians of this world that they are wrong, though I wouldn't be truthful if I said that wasn't a common temptation or thought. It's about the mission. We live in a changing world. Many say that the church is in decline; some say we need CPR. When I think about CPR, I don't care if it's a man or a woman doing it! We simply need to join God in his grand rescue operation, and we need all hands on deck. We need both men and women with dirt under their fingernails. We need men and women on the road to proclamation. A mission is at hand; it's time to get on with it.

When women are held back from using their gifts simply because of their gender, the people of God will continue to be hampered and not live into the fullness of the mission we have been invited into. Friends, there is a mission before us, and we must get our act together. This, then, is not merely a *justice* issue; rather, it's a *mission* issue.

EIGHT

AN EMBOLDENED
IMAGINATION

SITTING IN MY OFFICE is a beautiful teal box full of paper clips. Although I don't keep paper files, I do use the clips to attach my sermon outlines into my Bible for Sunday mornings. Not too long ago, my youngest son, Noah, found some paper clips on the floor of our house. When he found them he yelled, "Mommy, your sermon clips are on the ground!"[1]

When my boys visit my office—after filling their pockets with candy from all the candy dishes in the administrative office—they almost always make their way to the teal box on my desk. They love to open the box, pull out the paper clips, and let their imaginations run wild. Noah loves to make necklaces, while Caleb loves to build elaborate robots or rocket ships. When they get their hands on paper clips, they know they are Mommy's "sermon clips," but that doesn't stop their imaginations from using the paper clips in creative ways. To them, paper clips can't be boxed in; their uses are endless.

Why have adult imaginations become so limited? Someday my boys will stop making beautiful pieces of art out of paper clips; someday they will see them for what they are—paper clips. Similarly, because women rarely teach, preach, and lead from up front, our imaginations will continue to be limited. When women don't teach, preach, and lead, we will continue to put them into the teal boxes of our churches: neat, quiet, and safe. Young girls sitting in the pews will never come out of their boxes, get their hands dirty, and boldly go where few have gone in their generation. Something happens to our imaginations when women preach: women in the pews come alive. When women teach, preach, and lead, women in the pews begin to open their confined imaginations and undo the narrative that their role exists in a perfectly fitted box.

OLD BARRIERS CRUMBLE

In a world of male church and parachurch leaders, I can recall many instances during my childhood when I tried to figure out where I fit into the picture. At one time in my childhood I asked my mother if a woman could be a senior pastor. I didn't ask because someone had hit me over the head with a Bible verse telling me I couldn't, but I had never seen a woman teach, preach, pastor, or lead. Later on in my teen years, when I still wasn't sure if I was allowed to preach or if it was a ladylike thing to do, I decided that I should marry a pastor so I could be on mission in a local church. Perhaps then I could preach, teach, and lead in the confines of a women's ministry while my husband led the church. For years, I had difficulty seeing it any other way. When women aren't on mission alongside of their brothers, the imagination of the bride of Christ is hindered—it can imagine only half of what it might be.

The point is this: Women teaching, preaching, and leading today are not only important for the present church but also for the future church, for our sons and daughters. By encouraging our sons' and daughters' imagination now, we will see more men and women rise up together for the sake of the gospel. When women teach, lead, minister, evangelize, and preach, there is a ground swell, an uprising. Barriers are torn down, and the once-silenced mouths are opened. When women teach, lead, minister, evangelize, and preach, the church's imagination is expanded and *made new*. Not only this, but we participate in something much bigger than ourselves. We stand in the middle of the grandest story ever told—that is, the story of God.

Even in churches that affirm women in ministry, many women sit in the pews on Sunday morning unsure what to do with Scriptures that tell them to "keep quiet in the church." It's not uncommon for a young woman to come to me and ask about some of those tough passages. Without being taught the proper way to read Scripture, or without ever seeing a woman teach, preach, and lead, many women remain content with the same old narrative that tells them to keep quiet. However, when a woman stands behind the pulpit, opens the Word of God, and begins to proclaim the truth in a way that only she can, or when women are seen leading, praying publically, or doing things that they aren't often seen doing, other women are pushed to think critically about those tough passages. They are pushed to consider their own gifts. They are forced to ponder a false narrative they have embraced for far too long—that they are somehow less capable or less gifted than men in the kingdom of God.

When a woman teaches, preaches, leads, organizes, and evangelizes, other women see a supernatural talent empowered by the Spirit and propelled to edify *all of the people of God*. And it is then that women in the congregation begin to ask, Can I preach too? Maybe they will unearth the talents that have been buried too long; maybe they will spread their wings and fly; maybe they too will use their gifts in new and inspiring ways.

After just a few months at PazNaz, I began to build friendships with some amazing women. Many of the women at PazNaz have been encouraged to finally have a woman as their pastor, and some have been pondering their own role within the body of Christ. One young woman in particular is a very successful business woman with loads of leadership talent and genius. One day after hearing my story of preaching to the cornfields when I was a teenager, she nervously pulled me aside to share her story: "I completely forgot about this and haven't thought about it in years, but I used to preach to my bushes when I was a little girl." She shared how her imagination was once limitless for her role within the body of Christ, but somewhere along the way it was placed back in the little teal box. I am not suggesting that she has disobeyed God, but I can't help but wonder what her life would be like if she had been planted in soil rich with imagination for men and women in the church. Interestingly, this young woman has been revisiting her old imagination. She's been pulling it out of the little teal box and is nurturing it yet again. She just enrolled in classes at a local Christian school and is going to "see what God does." Something profound happens when women teach, preach, and lead! The future of the church is expanded, the imagination of many are fed, and more hands are on deck.

Similarly, one morning after our second worship service, a mom and a young girl (age seven or eight) were standing in line to greet me; I could see them waiting for a while. When I finally got to them the mom said, "This is my daughter, and she's never seen a female pastor before, and she really wanted to meet you." Holding back tears, I bent down and said, "It's pretty amazing to see women teaching, preaching, and leading, isn't it?" There's no telling what God might have in store for her, but the opportunities, I pray and hope, will be endless. That day, this little girl's imagination came out of the teal box. That day, she saw a place for herself in body of Christ.

OUR IMAGINATIONS ARE EXPANDED
TO REFLECT GOD'S STORY

When I was sixteen years old, I endeavored to read my Bible cover to cover. It was during this time that I surrendered my life to King Jesus. But in particular, I can remember reading the stories of Deborah and Esther, and feeling emboldened to be a fearless female leader. I also remember the first time I read through the Gospel of John as a teenager. When I arrived at John's Gospel and read about Mary being emboldened to proclaim the resurrection, my imagination was expanded. As a young woman reading that passage, I quickly shot up from my bed and began to pace around my room in excitement. I shouted. I prayed. I thanked God. And I began to see differently my role in God's kingdom.

Though the leadership of some churches is no longer exclusively male and women are included in the mix, we should realize that today's women preachers, teachers, and leaders aren't the first trailblazers. In the early church women like Junia also participated in the mission of God (see Rom 16:7). Women on mission alongside of their brothers are the Junias of our day. Scot McKnight explains,

> Junia, my friends, is not alone. Many women today are active in ministry and are continuing with confidence and power the storied history of women in the Bible and the silenced history of women in the church. They are not silenced as they once were, and so we look around and sing to the women among us who are embodying the gifts God has given to them.[2]

These women were called by God, gifted by the empowering presence of the Spirit, and employed to encourage the people of God in big and bold ways. When women are emboldened to preach, lead, or minister, they carry the legacy of Phoebe, Priscilla, Mary, Junia, Deborah, Huldah, Miriam, and Esther. Women stand among the priesthood of *all believers* and the Christological proclamation in Galatians 3:28.

In Mark 1:15, Jesus declared, "The time has come. The kingdom of God has come near. Repent and believe the good news!" This kingdom is one that breaks in to restore, heal, save, liberate, and strip the powers of death, darkness, and patriarchy. This in-breaking power of God's kingdom inaugurated and fulfilled in Christ is inclusive and on display for all. Men, women, Jew, Gentile, slaves, and free are all invited to the table, to the feast. Those who respond to the words of Jesus become the *new creation*, the *new community*, and the *family of God*. And those who call themselves brothers and sisters in

Christ are equally emboldened to announce the goodness of God's kingdom!

WOMEN SEE THEY ARE INVITED TO THE TABLE

One time I received a handwritten letter from a twenty-something who is wildly in love with Jesus and her local church, but is also wildly confused. She writes,

> I'm really wrestling with God's view of women, and what role my life is. It's really hard for me as a new believer to be able to intellectually and biblically understand why women are treated as they are in American churches. It's hard to piece apart what is biblical and what is sinful patriarchy warping Scripture to keep women in their place. . . . Are we just a subplot in a men's game? Did God really create me for a greater purpose that isn't just what man I belong to?

Sadly, this young woman is not alone in her discouragement and confusion. She doesn't see a narrative of the church inviting her to the table. Her imagination is limited. She is one of the brightest young people I have ever met; she graduated from an Ivy League school when she was only twenty years old. She is spunky; she is talented; she is gifted. When I watch her, it's hard for me not to imagine all the ways her gifts could be used to edify the church. I could see her as a teacher, a writer, a theologian, a seminary professor, or a pastor. But, sadly, she doesn't see a seat at the table for her.

When women are not sidelined, young women—much like the one who wrote this letter—begin to imagine what it would be like to sit at the table, and through their imaginations they are empowered and then edified. Again, when women teach, lead, minister, evangelize, and preach, there is a ground swell, an uprising. Barriers are torn down, and the once-silenced mouths are opened. When women teach, lead, minister, evangelize, and preach, the church's imagination is expanded and *made new*. Other women are given the confidence that they are not only *able* but also *called* to use their gifts within the body of Christ.

A sixteen-year-old woman was trying to make sense of the world after her parents had a nasty divorce. She was broken. But through a parachurch organization, she heard the good news of King Jesus, and her life was transformed. She had a sense of purpose and eventually a call to ministry. Within that parachurch organization, many young female campus ministers allowed her to imagine what her calling could look like. Both men and women mentored her, discipled her, and brought her through the process until she landed her dream job as a campus minister to high school students. Her imagination wasn't limited because she saw early on what it looked like for men and women to serve together—without subordination— for the good of God's kingdom. This, dear sisters, is what King Jesus calls us to be for others.

DON'T STOP EXPANDING YOUR IMAGINATION

My imagination has had to be expanded many times since I have been in ministry. Just when I am confident in my own calling and identity as a female pastor, something happens that makes it difficult for me to imagine my role. When I was serving as a high school youth pastor and teaching pastor at a church in the western suburbs of Chicago, I found out I was pregnant.

I'll never forget sitting in the office of my senior pastor explaining to him how "sorry I was" for being pregnant. With tears streaming down my face, I assured him over and over that "nothing will change" and I "promise I'll still be a good pastor."

My stunned and dumbfounded senior pastor got up from his desk, came around to where I was sitting, and gave me the biggest hug with the biggest smile on his face. "There is nothing to be sad about, Tara Beth, this is cause for celebration!" It wasn't that I wasn't happy to welcome a new child in the world, but I had zero imagination for a pastor who was a mom, let alone a preacher with a big ol' belly!

And leading up to my due date, I continued to preach twice a month, even with a massively growing belly. Of course, every time I was finished with a sermon and greeted folks on their way out, they didn't want to talk about my sermon but about my belly. One Sunday a gentleman said, "I could really only focus on some of your sermon, but most of the time all I could think about was your giant belly and if I would ever see your little guy kick." As my pregnancy progressed, my imagination for being a pastor and a mom dwindled to almost nothing. I continued to tell myself these stories:

- You can't be effective with a giant belly.
- Your belly is just a distraction.
- When you have the baby, you can't be effective.
- You can't be a good mom and a good pastor.
- Your fellow pastors are disappointed in you for having a baby.

- Once this baby comes, it's all people will want to talk about.
- People are going to judge you for choosing to continue in ministry after the baby is born.
- You're going to lose your passion for ministry as soon as the baby comes.
- You'll definitely lose any cool factor you had, and you'll soon just be another soccer mom driving a minivan.

I repeated these often. But right around the time I was thirty-nine weeks pregnant, I picked up Nancy Beach's book *Gifted to Lead.* As I read her book, every page was covered in tears. Nancy expanded my imagination yet again for women in ministry. She encouraged me to see that pregnancy was not a nail in the coffin for women in ministry. She unfolded her journey as a mother and teaching pastor at one of the world's largest churches. And over time I have slowly embraced an imagination for women in ministry that includes a baby on one hip.

To this day, one of my favorite family pictures is from my installation as senior pastor at First Church of the Nazarene of Pasadena. As we were being introduced to the congregation, I, in my black suit and heels, proudly held my four-year-old on my hip, while my six-year-old stood by my side with disheveled hair, partially tucked-in shirt, tummy totally hanging out, and a crooked tie. To me, this picture was the not-so-perfect but just-how-it-should-be picture of a mama in ministry. Right before that photo was taken, my boys were handed $2 bills to remember this moment, and my four-year-old, Noah, marched over to one of the candles on the Communion Table and tried to light it on fire!

Then, during the prayer time, when the entire staff, board, and trustees surrounded our family for the laying on of hands, Noah decided that would be the perfect time to play peekaboo with the entire congregation. But when I look at this picture—with Noah on my hip and Caleb slightly disheveled—I now proudly embrace this beautiful image of pastoring and motherhood. And I pray this simple image gives us a glimpse into God's in-breaking kingdom, which is expanded to embolden men and women to the pulpit, even with a baby on one hip.

When women teach, preach, and lead, even with babies on their hip, the pews rumble, the ground begins to shift, barriers are torn down, and once-silenced mouths are opened. Other women are given the confidence that they are not only *able* but also *called* to use their gifts within the body of Christ.

Our imaginations should never stop expanding. I attended a fundraising banquet for a chapel of a nearby Christian school. Although I was there to support members of my church and to support the endeavor, I walked away with a fresh imagination for women in ministry. You would think that after twelve or so years of ministry and after months into my present pastorate I would have a well-formulated vision for women in ministry. I did and I do. But there are times when my imagination is like a dry and parched place. Grace was a pastor's wife whose imagination wasn't fully expanded until the passing of her husband. Suddenly, she was emboldened in a new way as she began preaching in pulpits across the western region of the United States. To many, she became a household name because of her impassioned preaching and clear teaching on the Word of God. At the banquet, two of her grandsons got up

and shared some of their favorite memories of Grandma
(Grace) Prescott. Grandma Prescott nurtured them with hugs,
Bible stories, and adventures in the front seat of the car as they
traveled to revivals. They shared stories of people who came
into her home and spoke of her world-famous rolls that she
blessed churches with. As I listened to these stories, I imagined
myself for the first time as a grandma and a minister. I
imagined continuing to bless others with the gift of hospitality
while still fiercely serving the bride of Christ. On that day, my
imagination was expanded.

As the bride of Christ, we must continue to press the boundaries of our imaginations for women's roles in the church.
Black, brown, white, old, young, rich, and poor are included
and called into this kingdom vision of Jesus. All are emboldened to proclaim the good news of the feast. Whether she
has a baby on her hip or is single or has blue hair or never had
babies, if she can teach, preach, and lead, embolden her to the
pulpit. When we do, something profound begins to rumble in
the pews, the ground begins to shift, barriers are torn down,
and the once-silenced mouths are opened. Other women are
given the confidence that they are not only *able* but also *called*
to use their gifts within the body of Christ.

NINE

EMBOLDENED
COLABORERS

THE CALIFORNIA BREEZE gently swept across the patio as the orange trees rustled in the backyard.[1] Jeff and I sat on the patio after just having finished a brunch fit for a king and queen. Living in blustery Chicago my whole life, it was hard for me to believe that we were sitting outdoors on February 26. Jeff and I sat with a dozen or more church board members who were interviewing me to be their lead pastor. To say the church was a historic church would almost be an understatement—it was *the flagship* church for the denomination. Phineas F. Bresee, the father of our denomination, planted it himself, and it was also one of the largest within the denomination. Historically, the church led the way by approaching the future with a missional boldness and a posture of humility and grace. But as we sat on the patio that day, this church was contemplating stepping onto a frontier that a church of that size in that denomination had *never* done before. As the head of the search committee, Larry opened the discussion during the second interview. There was tension in the air:

Tara Beth, when your name first came to me in the search process, I watched a sermon of yours and immediately knew that you were gifted, anointed, and called by God. As I thought about how I would bring your name forward to the search committee and congregation, I knew we would face obstacles and challenges. *This would be so much easier if she were a man!* I thought to myself. But then I felt the Holy Spirit whisper to me, "When have I ever called you to do the easy thing?" With that, I never looked back but began the process of bringing your name forward. So let's have a conversation about what it would mean for us to have a woman pastor.

Larry emboldens women. Throughout the entire call process, Larry knew that he might face ridicule and pushback, calling a woman would be hard, and it would be a challenge. But he relentlessly stuck to the task because he believed God was calling a woman to the church, and he obediently and courageously emboldened me to ministry.

MEN WHO EMBOLDEN WOMEN TAKE RISKS

Although my tradition affirms the role of women in ministry theologically, the rubber does not actually meet the road. As mentioned in the introduction of the book, the statistics are alarmingly lopsided when it comes to male leaders vis-à-vis female leaders in the church. Now let's put some flesh on this. When I graduated from college in 2004, I graduated with more than a dozen women who studied theology and ministry. In 2016, *only a couple of them were in ministry*, and I would assume that it was because *it's just too hard and too painful.* Being treated as a second-class citizen gets old; trying to navigate a walled-up male culture is exhausting; seeing terrible theology taught over and over is numbing; living up to the expectations of being homemaker, taxi driver for the family, homeroom mom, party planner extraordinaire, and family planner *on top of* being a full-time minister burns us out. So, for many women in ministry, the stakes are too high. And the brutal reality is that the stakes will continue to be too high until men turn their theology into practice. And putting this into practice begins with *taking risks.*

Men who take risks do it while fully aware that something significant is at stake—something much more significant than ridicule or fear. Men who take risks do it because *they realize that the church is at stake,* and until women are no longer sidelined, the church will continue to be hampered. Men who embolden women by taking risks recognize that the church has been limping along for far too long, and it's high time the status quo changes.

Let's take a look at Barnabas and Saul (later Paul) as examples. In Acts 9, a man named Saul had been breathing murderous threats against the early church. After his radical conversion experience and devoting his life to Christ, Saul is renamed Paul and begins preaching the good tidings of the gospel.

> Saul spent several days with the disciples in Damascus. At once he began to preach in the synagogues that Jesus is the Son of God. All those who heard him were astonished and asked, "Isn't he the man who raised havoc in

Jerusalem among those who call on this name? And hasn't he come here to take them as prisoners to the chief priests?" Yet Saul grew more and more powerful and baffled the Jews living in Damascus by proving that Jesus is the Messiah.

After many days had gone by, there was a conspiracy among the Jews to kill him, but Saul learned of their plan. Day and night they kept close watch on the city gates in order to kill him. But his followers took him by night and lowered him in a basket through an opening in the wall.

When he came to Jerusalem, he tried to join the disciples, but they were all afraid of him, not believing that he really was a disciple. *But Barnabas took him and brought him to the apostles.* He told them how Saul on his journey had seen the Lord and that the Lord had spoken to him, and how in Damascus he had preached fearlessly in the name of Jesus. So Saul stayed with them and moved about freely in Jerusalem, speaking boldly in the name of the Lord. He talked and debated with the Hellenistic Jews, but they tried to kill him. When the believers learned of this, they took him down to Caesarea and sent him off to Tarsus. (Acts 9:19-30, emphasis added)

There was much to fear about Paul. Understandably, the early church feared for their own lives, so naturally they questioned his intentions when he wanted to join them in the great mission of God. But one very bold disciple, led by the Spirit, took a risk and *emboldened Paul.* Imagine for a moment if Paul would have been held back. Imagine for a moment if Paul would have never been welcomed into the early church because of fear. Thankfully, Barnabas was not led by fear but by the Spirit.

This should go without being stated, but women are no threat to the church, although many say they are. We are not dangerous; we are certainly not breathing murderous threats, but much like Paul, we have a burning and fiery passion to preach the good news of Jesus Christ. And much like the early church feared Paul, a similar narrative of fear holds sway over women who seek to lead alongside their brothers. The fear of the unknown, the fear of the "feminization of the church," the fear that women aren't strong enough, the fear that women are too weak to lead, the fear that a woman's voice in the pulpit will be difficult to listen to, the fear that people will leave the community, and the fear that a woman can't possibly lead and be a mother: these are just a *few* of the fears that keep women chained to the sidelines. But hear this again: "Barnabas took him and brought him to the apostles. He told them how Saul on his journey had seen the Lord and that the Lord had spoken to him, and how in Damascus he had preached fearlessly in the name of Jesus" (v. 27).

There was much to lose when Barnabas brought Paul to the apostles, but there was *much more to lose by not bringing him to the apostles.* Brothers in Christ, it can be risky to embolden your sister in Christ. You might be ridiculed. You might cause uproar. You might see people leave your church. You might see pastors leave your denomination. You might lose some of your biggest givers. How much longer will you be a slave to fear? When will you start bringing women before your congregations and faithfully proclaim that the bride of Christ will continue to limp along until we *embolden gifted, called, and anointed* women in our midst?

MEN WHO EMBOLDEN MENTOR

It's true. Colaboring men and women together can at times be awkward. What are the boundaries? Can we be together in an office alone? Should there be windows in the office? Should we leave the door open? If we have a lunch meeting, do we have to drive in separate cars? What about texting and emails, should other people be copied? Can we meet together at a restaurant alone for lunch?

The parachurch ministry of my youth had very strict boundaries on cross-gender relationships, especially among staff. Men and women *never* were to meet alone, drive together alone, or be seen together alone. There was much to fear and much to lose—for many, the gospel was at stake. Moral failures of the past were whispered in the cubicles to remind one another of the severe danger of cross-gender relationships. As a young woman in ministry, boundaries made sense, but it wasn't until years later that I began to see how inhibiting these boundaries can be.

While boundaries are important, at times we set boundaries that are unsustainable and even impossible for women in leadership. In our highly sexualized culture, the knee-jerk reaction is to view women as dangerous temptresses and men as animals who can't control themselves. Certainly, when cross-gender relationships go awry, there's a lot to lose. We hear, for example, of a senior pastor who ran off with the choir director. No doubt, many churches have been deeply wounded due to this kind of scandal. It's scary and it's devastating. So naturally, to protect ourselves from moral failure, strict boundaries and high walls are created. A protective posture, of course, is a natural instinct hardwired in our bodies. Sometimes, we can't help it. But when boundaries, rules, and high walls become the primary way we choose to lead with and relate to one another, it becomes increasingly more difficult for men to embolden women in ministry. Leading this way can quickly exclude women from the table.

As more women are called into leadership positions in the church, a culture of strict boundaries will penalize women due to their gender. In a culture of strict boundaries, we communicate to women that they are untrustworthy or even shameful simply because of the shape of their body. In her book *Dare Mighty Things*, Halee Gray Scott sketches polar-opposite approaches often seen in churches. She calls the extreme boundary approach the "bubble-wrap approach."[2] This approach, popularized by Billy Graham, includes never being alone with a woman without a third party present. While this approach has many strengths, the long-term impact on women has been detrimental. When a church culture is dominated by men, and when they see these harsh boundaries as the only path to maintaining personal purity, women will continue to remain on the fringes of leadership.

Halee Gray Scott goes on to call the second approach the "daredevil approach," which lands on the opposite end of the spectrum from the bubble-wrap approach. Here there are few boundaries for cross-gender relationships.[3] According to Scott, those who follow the daredevil approach give no thought to extravagant gift giving over the holidays, vacations, and fancy dinners within cross-gender relationships. The dangers in this approach should be obvious, and the resulting temptations can become too much to bear. Scott compares this approach to swimming in the ocean without knowing the force and direction of the undertow.[4]

Men who embolden women in ministry must be willing to mentor them. In a mentoring relationship a wiser person guides a less-experienced person—often a younger colleague or student—through advice, training, time, and often one-on-one conversations. Mentoring can't happen when the boundaries are so strict that it excludes women from the table, and mentoring also can't happen when the lack of boundaries creates too much risk and temptation. Knowing that men who embolden women must be willing to mentor women, I would like to propose a few foundational points before mentoring women:

1. Know your boundaries before going into a relationship. I fully acknowledge that some boundaries might be different for different people. Whatever your boundaries are, let them come out of wisdom, prayer, and discernment, not fear. If you feel the need to express your boundaries to your mentee, then do so. But don't make things more awkward and uncomfortable than they need to be.

2. If you feel like you need to hide a relationship from anyone, especially your spouse, then that should be a clear red flag that something's not right.

3. Tend to your relationship with Jesus first and foremost, as well as your relationship with your spouse. If suddenly

your mentoring relationship becomes a priority, something is out of balance.

4. Allow the spouses of the mentee and mentor to talk to one another about the relationship.

We must create a new culture that does not keep women sidelined due to gender, especially in our churches. This means men who embolden women must be willing to mentor women. One doesn't have to read far in the New Testament to see that women played significant roles as teachers, prophets, evangelists, apostles, and ministering widows. They were, of course, serving in cross-gender, colaboring relationships. Just a few of these examples are Mary Magdalene, Joanna, and Susanna, who provided for the disciples (Lk 8:1-3); Mary and Martha, who opened their home to Jesus and served his needs in a very personal way; and Priscilla and Aquila, who taught Apollos and served the kingdom as colaborers with Paul (Acts 18:24-28; Rom 16:3-4; 1 Cor 16:19).

MEN WHO EMBOLDEN TEACH

When the average person in the pew comes across difficult passages such as 1 Timothy 2:11-12, they are typically confused by its meaning and context. Without proper education and solid biblical teaching, many in your congregation will remain confused (or worse) without a proper hermeneutic and understanding of the problem passages, and women will remain silenced in our churches. Far too many pastors who affirm women in ministry assume that people in their pews are on the same page. Sadly, this could not be any further from reality.

Here is a confession from Bill Hybels at a recent Global Leadership Summit.

> Somewhere in the middle 90s, I think, I said, I don't have to carry that flag anymore. Because the whole church gets it; we are done with that. We've crossed over. In the last ten years, I am embarrassed to say, it's gone the other way. There is a generation of leaders coming up now who are back in the old school of limiting the potential of what women can do; limiting where women can serve; limiting their potential service in the church. I don't get it. But I freely admit that I misjudged where I thought the church was going. Corporations are way in front of us, universities, my gosh the military is in front of us. And churches are lagging behind on this. If I could do it over again, I would have kept the pressure up until every last church that I could influence would allow women to serve, and to use their gifts, and to be full image bearers in the church.[5]

Bill's words were no doubt timely, helpful, and needed. I am grateful he used his platform to speak out on such an important subject. Too many pastors are unwilling to make such a confession. Although many pastors almost always have the best intentions, countless women are discouraged, frustrated, and even walk away from their call to ministry. Men who embolden women boldly and clearly teach the full inclusion of women in ministry; men who embolden women "put the pressure up until every last church . . . allow[s] women to serve, and use their gift."[6] Bill confesses that somewhere along the line he stopped carrying the ball down the field, and more churches must recognize this fumble.

If a pastor rarely teaches the stories of Junia, Phoebe, Deborah, Priscilla, and Mary; and if the pastor rarely tells the stories of women in the early days of his denomination; and if the pastor rarely teaches some of the problem passages in the New Testament, the people in the congregation will lose sight of the kingdom imagination for women in the church. Therefore, people in the congregation will get their information from scholars and pastors who don't affirm women in ministry. Men who embolden women don't wait before it's too late to paint the kingdom vision for women in the church; they do it as if it's second nature. Men who embolden women paint the kingdom vision for women in the church with such vigor, color, and beauty that women in their pews imagine a world in which they are invited to the table to use their gifts and soar with great freedom.

MEN WHO EMBOLDEN KEEP WOMEN VISIBLE IN LEADERSHIP

JR. Forasteros, a pastor in Dallas, Texas, does this better than any pastor I've ever met. From the first time I met him, this burly, tattooed, hipster pastor has been passionate about emboldening women in the kingdom. Because it's second nature to him, he doesn't find it a challenge to spot women who are ready to lead. JR. says this to fellow male leaders:

If you're in church leadership (vocationally or as a lay person), you have influence. You have a platform. Use that privilege to create spaces for women to lead—and not just in the Kids' Ministry or on the Hospitality team.

If you're fortunate enough to lead a hiring process, you can specifically seek out women. Ordained women are grossly underemployed. There are hundreds of gifted and called women who cannot get ministry positions. Hire them.

You may not be in a position to hire, but that doesn't mean your hands are tied. At Catalyst Church, where I co-pastor, I created a lay preaching team, and we currently have two women preaching regularly (3-4 times per year each). Several more women are part of the team that edits each of my sermons before I preach them.

Our leadership team has 2 women of 5 total members and we regularly feature video stories of men and women in our congregation sharing how they are responding to God's calling in their lives.

Spotting a woman who is ready to lead isn't difficult. They attend your church. If you can't think of any way to equip them, ask them. Say, "What do you wish you could do as a part of our Church?" Then work together to figure out how to make it happen.[7]

Whenever I have a conversation with JR., he beams with pride for all of the ways he is intentional about emboldening women in leadership. JR. gets it. He gets the importance of young women seeing other women be in visible roles of leadership within the church. JR. gets that when women lead, teach, pastor, evangelize, disciple, and preach, other younger women begin to undo the narrative that tells them they are *inferior to men*. JR. understands that when women lead, teach, pastor, evangelize, disciple, and preach, other women are pushed to think critically about those tough passages; they are pushed to consider their own gifts; they are forced to ponder the false narrative they have embraced far too long—that they are somehow less capable or less gifted in the kingdom of God. JR. sees that when women are emboldened, other women see a supernatural talent embodied in another woman, empowered by the Spirit, and propelled to edify *all of the people of God*. And then women in the congregation begin to ask, "Can I lead too?" Maybe they will unearth the talents that have been long buried; maybe they will spread their wings and fly; maybe they too will use their gifts in new and inspiring ways.

JR. gets it that when women teach, preach, lead, evangelize, pastor, and disciple, we get a glimpse of the kingdom vision for men and women in the church.

THE APOSTLE PAUL EMBOLDENED WOMEN

In the conclusion to his letter to the Romans, Paul lists a group of people he is thankful for. These women were courageous colaborers of the gospel who "risked their lives" for Paul (Rom 16:4). Not only does Paul have a notable group of women but he does something rather unusual for his time. When listing a husband and wife, a husband's name was almost always listed before his wife's name. But Paul more than once writes Priscilla's name before her husband's (Acts 18:18-19, 26; Rom 16:3; 2 Tim 4:19). Priscilla was an educated woman, a gifted teacher, and along with her husband is called Paul's coworker. Priscilla and her husband colabored with Paul by leading, teaching, and preaching. Of course, Priscilla is just one of the many women who colabored with Paul, but Paul *didn't have to write Priscilla's name before her husband's*. Paul *could have* given into the cultural norm and written her husband's name *first*, but he didn't. Paul gave visibility to Priscilla, and although we will never fully know the reason, it is likely because she had a notable leadership role in Paul's network. No doubt about it, Priscilla was an active, prominent, and courageous laborer for the gospel, and Paul both knew it and acknowledged it. Paul emboldened women.

In conclusion, the following are practical steps that men and churches can implement to move from only affirming women to empowering them in ministry:

1. Go out of your way to affirm gifted women in your midst.

2. If you notice a woman who is gifted, come alongside her and help her find resources for equipping and encouragement.

3. If you notice a woman in a meeting staying quiet, specifically ask for her thoughts.

4. Mentor women.

5. Resist male-only friendships; it excludes women and creates a good-ol'-boys club mentality.

6. If you're a preacher, tell stories of women in your sermons.

7. If you're a preacher, preach on the kingdom vision for men and women in ministry at least once a year.

8. Invite women pastors to the decision-making table.

9. Refuse a male-only platform. Look to Christian Community Development Association and Missio Alliance, which always have diverse platforms.

10. If you're in a place to hire, work hard to have an equal number of male and female candidates.

11. Refuse tokenism.

The time isn't tomorrow, next month, or next year, dear brothers, but now. Now is the time to regularly teach the full inclusion of women in leadership. Now is the time to mentor a woman in your midst. Now is the time to make women visible on the platform and refuse a male-only platform or culture. Now is the time to embrace the kingdom vision of Jesus and the apostle Paul. Dear brothers, now is the time to reclaim the kingdom vision for gifted women in the church.

TEN

AN EMBOLDENED CHURCH

FRANCES WILLARD WAS A WELL-KNOWN LEADER in the nineteenth-century temperance movement, but also deep down within her soul bellowed a longing for men and women together to be emboldened.[1] As a passionate evangelist, she was eventually invited to join Dwight L. Moody during his Boston campaign.[2] However, there was a growing opposition to her ministry, and the tour was short-lived. For just a blip on the kingdom-vision radar, Frances Willard and Dwight L. Moody were colaboring for the sake of the mission. Although she had to step back from her side-by-side role with Moody, she never stopped advocating for her fellow sisters in Christ: "Let me as a loyal daughter of the church, urge upon younger women who feel a call, as I once did, to preach the unsearchable riches of Christ."[3] Not only did she desire to see women emboldened to the pulpit, but she longed to see men *and* women *together* emboldened to the pulpit. In a letter to Mrs. Moody, Willard shared this kingdom vision:

> All my life I have been devoted to the advancement of women in education and opportunity, I firmly believe

God has a work for them to do as evangelists, as bearers of Christ's message to the ungospeled, to the prayer-meeting, to the church generally and the world at large, such as most people have not dreamed. It is therefore my dearest wish to help break down barriers of prejudice that keep them silent. I cannot think that meetings in which "the brethren" only are called upon, are one half as effective as those where all are freely invited, and I can believe that "women's meetings," as such, are a relic of an outworn regime. Never did I hold one of these meetings without a protest in my soul against it. As in the day of Pentecost, so now, let men and women in perfectly impartial fashion participate in all services conducted in His name in whom there is neither bond nor free, male nor female, but all are one.[4]

Willard's longing was the kingdom vision of an emboldened church. A church, when truly emboldened, is one where there are no spectators, but everyone has an instrument and sings the emboldened song. An emboldened church can be likened to a symphony that I wrote about a few years ago:

For most of my life I have played the cello. The sound radiating from the instrument when the bow is drawn across the strings is exquisite. I enthusiastically admit my bias, as I claim the cello to be the most beautiful instrument in the world. As a solo performer, the cello has no equal, but as incredible as it is on its own, there is nothing as captivating as an entire symphony orchestra with all types of strings, woodwinds, brass, and percussion contributing to the mosaic of sound. When the conductor raises his hands and the instruments are pulled up and into position, magic begins.

When I was a senior in high school, our symphony orchestra entered into a statewide competition. Our conductor carefully selected a piece that he believed suited our orchestra well, "The Overture from Egmont" by Ludwig van Beethoven. Never before had I played something so profound . . . so poetic . . . so magical. The first time I heard Beethoven's masterpiece, I could not hold back my tears.

Sheet music was distributed to our ensemble and we went to work. I practiced day and night, but performing alone never had the same impact on my emotions as when we played together. The cello role, while exciting, seemed incomplete when played by itself. The first time we played it together as an entire symphony orchestra was unlike anything I had ever experienced as a young musician. I laughed with joy during some movements and wept in others. The magic was created by the simultaneous contribution of eighty musicians moving at the same pace, creating the music that Ludwig van Beethoven created in his head, generated by his heart. If the cello was removed, we would have lost the haunting melody that sang underneath the violins. If the wind section was taken away, we would have lost the joyful melody that only wind instruments can bring. Remove any part and it destroys the whole.

Beethoven did not write his Overture from Egmont with one instrument in mind, but he also didn't create it so that every instrument would sound exactly the same. The mystique of it all is that Beethoven wrote the symphony with all the instruments in mind and for each instrument to shine in the way that only each can sing in their very own way. The beauty of music happens when the ensemble comes together in one unifying voice.[5]

Remove women from a seat at the table and it destroys the whole. Remove women from teaching, preaching, and leading, and the beauty of the music is limited.

When I was considering coming to PazNaz, I met the executive pastor, Scott Anderson, during the interview and discernment process. Scott had served with the former pastor for twelve years, and they were quite the powerful duo. Before coming, many warned me that there would be a host of problems having an executive pastor used to serving alongside a male pastor much older than me; loyalty issues might surface. So when I met Scott, I was nervous. Would it work? Would there be sabotage? Could he work with a thirty-four-year-old female senior pastor? Would he be open to helping execute change? I met Scott on a sunny March morning in Southern California. He pulled up in his white BMW convertible with his silver hair flowing in the wind. His fashion and design sense coupled with his savvy skills with numbers, Excel spreadsheets, and administration is a fun combo. But I wasn't sure if that would translate to working with me.

When we sat down over breakfast, the chemistry was almost instant. We talked mission, philosophy, ministry models, and vision. But it wasn't that we were on the same page for the future of the church that stood out to me, it was his humility and his deep, abiding love for Jesus. Now that we've been partnering together officially at PazNaz, I couldn't ask for a more emboldened partnership. I am transparent; Scott is cautious. I am a bold visionary; Scott keeps us grounded. I can imagine the future; Scott sees the numbers and execution to get us there. Not a decision is made without mutual discernment and discussion, and vision isn't cast without both of our prayers and discussion. If I have an idea, it's practically done before I even blink my eyes. When meeting with a disgruntled person, Scott tends to be matter-of-fact, while I tend to be more nurturing. Scott Anderson is more than an executive pastor, he is a close partner in ministry. Sometimes he's a string bass and I'm a violin, and sometimes he's beating the drum and I'm playing the trombone. The point is this: Scott and I are living out the emboldened mission together. PazNaz beautifully depicts an emboldened church. With just about as many female pastors as male pastors, both voices are represented in meetings, in decisions, and on the platform.

The emboldened church can't sing the symphony with only half the church—we need everyone to pick up an instrument and play the melody. Brothers and sisters in Christ, hear me: I need you, and you need me; we need you, and you need us. This, dear brothers and sisters, is an emboldened church.

I will say it yet again; this time let it settle in:

I need you.

You need me.

We need you.

You need us.

I need you to embolden me when imposter syndrome gets the best of me. *I need you* to come alongside me to walk this kingdom mission together. And *you need me* to walk alongside you, to encourage you, to push you, to sharpen you, to pray for you, and to rub shoulders with you. *You need me* to offer a perspective that represents over half of those sitting in the pews. And *we need you* to not hold back; rather, *we need you* to use your gifts as the apostle Paul commanded in Romans 12. *We need you* to teach, preach, serve, give generously, lead, prophesy, encourage, and heal. And don't forget, *you need us*. You and I, brothers and sisters, have a special bond that cannot be broken—we are bound by the love of the Father, the faithfulness of King Jesus, and the empowering presence of the Spirit. This kingdom mission isn't to be a stagnant, secluded, individualized mission, but one which beckons all who are spectators and pulls them into the mission at hand. This kingdom mission is a special calling to be lived out as colaborers— that is, men and women together, arm in arm, pushing one another, creatively using their own gifts to edify the other for mission.

I need your preaching, teaching, and leading, and you need mine. I need to break bread with you, and you with me. I need your conversation, and you need mine. I need you in my life, and you need me in yours. I need a seat at the table, and so do you. You don't have to do this alone. You can't. We can only do this as an emboldened church on this kingdom mission. I need you, you need me, we need you, and you need us. Together— arm in arm—we are an emboldened church, just as we were designed to be.

FIRST CHURCH OF THE EMBOLDENED

Welcome to First Church of the Emboldened. An emboldened church is not an elite club. At First Church of the Emboldened, we believe everyone matters—not just to fill a seat but to equip everyone for mission. At First Church of the Emboldened we believe *we* are what God chooses to use to change the world. God's light shines through an entire people, and God's presence is known through an entire people.

When you come, no one is sidelined; rather, every week we *all* use our gifts to edify and strengthen one another. Thus, during the rest of the week, God's presence and light shines brightly through us and others are drawn to join. Some of us might use our gifts to love a sick congregant. And some of us might discover we have the gift of proclaiming God's Word. We at the First Church of the Emboldened will help everyone grow in their gifts. Whatever our gifts are, they are needed, for an entire mission is on the line. We need every single person. Yes, you; you matter.

And here is the most magnificent thing about First Church of the Emboldened: Your gender isn't a qualifier for any particular place in our church. If you have the gift to lead and you are a female, get in the game and preach on, sister. If you have the gift of hospitality and love the kitchen, get in the game and get cooking, dear brother. At First Church of the Emboldened we embrace the emboldening and empowering presence of the Spirit of Pentecost, and we take very seriously the apostle Peter's words on the day of Pentecost, "your sons and daughters shall prophesy." We celebrate biblical women such as Deborah, the fearless leader; Huldah, the prophet who helped reignite

Israel's faith; Miriam, the gifted musician for the people of God; and Esther, the brave queen who seized the moment and boldly approached the king. We regularly lift up the names of Phoebe, a deacon and financial sponsor for Paul's missions; Priscilla, the gifted preacher; Mary, the mother of Jesus; and Junia, the bright and respected apostle. These women matter to us. They are emboldened women, and at First Church of the Emboldened, we believe we have both Junias and Pauls in our midst, so let's work together. We are on a mission.

IT'S NOT AN ELITE SPORT

When I was in seventh grade, I used to sit in the gym bleachers every morning and watch the girls' volleyball team practice their bumps, sets, and spikes. Every morning I sat in awe of the fierceness of these players. Every once in a while a girl from the team would spike the ball so hard that it would hit the back wall of the gym and make a loud boom, which caused all the spectators to "ooh" and "aah." As I watched the players I would often daydream that I was on the court spiking the ball. My imagination was free to see myself as one of the players, but I was on the court *only* in my imagination.

The following year I decided to practice daily and try out for the team. I played as best as I could, I spiked as hard as I could, set as swiftly as I could, and I bumped as precisely as I could. But it wasn't enough, I didn't make the team. That, however, was okay—that is how elite teams work. The best of the best make the team, and those who don't make the team try to find a sport that best suits them. Churches, however, should not be an elite team sport—at least if it's going to be an emboldened church. The empowering presence of the Spirit is not selective; rather, the empowering and emboldening presence of the Spirit propels and impels *all* the people of God toward mission. To be sure, we have different roles—that is, some teach, preach, and lead, while others love to use their gifts of hospitality, but all are moving toward the same mission.

You, dear sisters and brothers, are called and commissioned to participate in God's grand mission. Yes, you. You are *perfectly wired* for this—in the Spirit, you have been given all that you need. So, dear church, don't squander these gifts. These gifted women and men in your midst are critical to your future. Without them, your future is dim.

When the apostle Paul wrote his first letter to the Corinthians, he had a deep and abiding concern for all to get in the game, not just the elite, and especially not just a single gender. Paul longed to see a unified church, always growing, always building, and always edifying one another with the gifts of the Spirit. Paul says in 1 Corinthians 14:12, "So it is with you. Since you are eager for gifts of the Spirit, try to excel in those that build up the church." These gifts include teaching, admonishing, prophesying, knowledge, exhortation, healing, miracles, and guidance. First Corinthians 12:4-11, for example, says,

> There are different kinds of gifts, but the same Spirit distributes them. There are different kinds of service, but the same Lord. There are different kinds of working, but in all of them and in everyone it is the same God at work.
>
> Now to each one the manifestation of the Spirit is given for the common good. To one there is given through

the Spirit a message of wisdom, to another a message of knowledge by means of the same Spirit, to another faith by the same Spirit, to another gifts of healing by that one Spirit, to another miraculous powers, to another prophecy, to another distinguishing between spirits, to another speaking in different kinds of tongues, and to still another the interpretation of tongues. All these are the work of one and the same Spirit, and he distributes them to each one, just as he determines.

In Paul's vision for the church, no one is on the sidelines. All of the gifts of the Spirit are given to male *and* female, not just men. The Holy Spirit doesn't pick genders! An emboldened church is a gifts-based church, not a gender-based one. In Paul's vision for the church, people are empowered by the Spirit to build up one another through these gifts, not as a solo performance or an elite sport, but more like a symphonic harmony—an emboldened church.

AN EMBOLDENED CHURCH INTENTIONALLY RIDES THE WAVE OF THE SPIRIT

Ever since I moved to California, I've been fascinated with the waves. Waves can teach us lessons about the nature of the Spirit. Of course, any analogy breaks down, especially when used of a person of the Trinity. Nevertheless, I am in awe of waves. Waves are powerful, a force to be reckoned with. And waves are always doing a *new thing*, a *unique thing*, and incredibly, waves do this without the help of humans. Waves roar and crash in their own power.

When I was in eighth grade, my family spent two weeks in Hawaii for a memorable vacation. The backdrop to the Hawaiian surf could be its own exhibit in any art museum. When waves roll to shore with the sun in the background, they sparkle as if adorned with diamonds. My brother, Travis, and I spent two weeks taking morning surf lessons on these exquisite waves. The first several days of lessons we didn't even get in the water; instead, we drilled on the sands of the beach. We learned the ins and the outs of the surfboard—how to carry it, how to paddle, how to stand on the board, and how to catch the perfect wave. Leo coached our every move on the sand so that when we would catch a wave for the first time, we'd be successful. The first time I paddled into the ocean was exhilarating. My coach wasn't going to let us fail. As I paddled out from shore, he reminded me of all the drills we had practiced on the beach and how to spot the perfect wave.

When the time came for me to face the shore and wait for the ultimate wave, Leo spoke words of encouragement; he believed in me. When the wave came his voice bellowed, "Go, Tara Beth, go! You've got this—paddle! Paddle!" I fiercely paddled as the wave, in its raw power, caught up to me. As I felt the wave begin to push my board and body forward, with the coach yelling in the background, I stood up and rode that wave to the shore. It was utterly exhilarating. I felt like this was exactly what I was destined to do that day. My success came because I was intentionally emboldened by a trained coach who prepared and empowered me to catch the wave. Yes, that moment took some preparation, practice, and effort on my part, but that moment happened because I was emboldened. Most importantly, I was caught up in the flow of the wave, but I still needed the coach to get me there. Without my coach, I likely would have flopped many times. And without the waves, there wouldn't be surfing.

When I think about riding the waves, I think about an emboldened church. I hear a lot of overspiritualization when folks talk about men and women in ministry. For example, not too long ago I shared with someone some of my discouragement with the lack of female pastors serving in churches. The gentleman looked at me and said, "We just need to trust God. Don't you believe that God is on the throne? Don't you think it was in God's perfect will to have the ministers pastor those congregations, whether they were male or female? What if God doesn't see gender?"

While I dearly love the bride of Christ, I also acknowledge we are far from the vision of the bride described in Revelation 21. We are broken and divisive at times, and I lament that we are still arguing over whether women can teach, preach, and lead. We need to embolden women to ride the wave of the Spirit. We can't sit and hope it happens—we need to coach, train, cheer, and empower women to catch the wave. If we aren't intentional about including, emboldening, equipping, training, and empowering those who are often excluded (women), there will hardly be a shift in the church's practice.

I ache for the day when the bride of Christ emboldens men *and* women to ride the waves of the Spirit without gender qualifiers. I long for the day when they look to the shore to see wide-eyed spectators watching them with longing and admiration. Then, on the shore, these Spirit-emboldened men and women grab spectators by the hand, look them in the eye, and boldly and lovingly affirm, "You too are surfers. You too can be emboldened. You too can ride the wave of the Spirit." Because the kingdom vision, which culminated in King Jesus, is that *no one is a spectator on the shores.*

The kingdom vision of Jesus beckons men and women alike to ride the waves together, cheering one another on, coaching one another, and using their own talents to sharpen others. The church is hardly emboldened when over half of its members are standing on the shore. In the emboldened church all are participating, and all are riding the waves of the Spirit. An emboldened church needs all hands on deck, hands of all shapes, sizes, races, genders, and backgrounds.

AN EMBOLDENED CHURCH IS A SIGN AND A WONDER

The church—that is, the people of God who live under the reign and rule of King Jesus—is to be a countercultural community that declares a drastic alternative to the world around them. In a world of pain, corruption, coercion, brokenness, division, and war, the church declares the radical alternatives of peace, generosity, love, healing, and unity. When the church lives a radical alternative to the world around them, it is a sign and wonder. God is doing a revolutionary thing in and through his people for all the world to see and recognize the wonder of God's goodness.

The church is a sign and wonder to the world when it is so awe-inspiring that others want to belong and live under King Jesus. The church then becomes a witness to the world that might prompt others to consider their lives. The reverse of the curse of the fall is one of the revolutionary things that has happened in Christ. And in the context of this book, this means the curse of men lording over women has been reversed.[6] Furthermore, anyone lording it over anyone else is reversed in Christ. Now we celebrate mutual submission. Therefore, the drastic alternative the church offers is one where men and women celebrate each others gifts, embolden one another, work shoulder to shoulder to participate in God's mission, and witness to the world what colaboring looks like.

Yes, I love the church, and my heart is burdened for the church. And in a world that suppresses and sidelines women, that sees women as sex objects, that unfairly pays women, and that unfairly criticizes women, the church has an opportunity to be a witness, to be a sign and a wonder in all of this. We have an opportunity to be a drastic alternative—to be a light. When the world is splitting hairs over pantsuits and fashion, the church is busy training, empowering, and emboldening women *and* men to preach and teach the most prized message in all of creation. The emboldened church sees women as important ministers, proclaimers, and leaders in God's kingdom. When the world peers into the emboldened church, they stand in awe of how women are empowered, and are challenged to think differently about how women are treated. This, you see, is a witness—a sign and a wonder.

Too many women in the church are peering into the world and seeing a better alternative for them—more opportunities, less sexism, and more empowerment. For this reason, dear ones, I have fire in my bones to see women on mission with their brothers. I have an ache in my soul to no longer see more men on the platform than women. I have a longing in my heart to see daughters have a new imagination for their role in the church. I have a hunger to see a new backdrop to our story—one that offers hope, freedom, empowerment, and unity for the bride of Christ.

BRIGHT HOPE FOR TODAY: PROFILES OF EMBOLDENED WOMEN

BISHOP MINERVA G. CARCAÑO

UMC.ORG/BISHOPS/MINERVA-G-CARCANO

Bishop Minerva G. Carcaño is the first Hispanic woman to be elected to the episcopacy of the United Methodist Church. She is one of fifty bishops leading more than eight million members in the UMC, and she advocates for the issue of immigration.

CHRISTENA CLEVELAND

CHRISTENACLEVELAND.COM

A preacher, social psychologist, theologian, researcher, author, and powerful communicator, Christena Cleveland speaks and writes widely on the intersection of justice and reconciliation. She is "in pursuit of a new reality in which all people have an empowered seat at the table, and there is no longer *us* and *them*—but simply us."

HELEN LEE

HELENLEEBOOKS.COM

A mom, publishing professional, author, and speaker, Helen Lee has been an influential and at times prophetic voice within evangelical Christianity. She has written widely, including her important book *The Missional Mom*. She is also an entrepreneur and was a cofounder of the Best Christian Workplaces.

ROBBIE CANSLER

HAMMONDMISSIONCHURCH.BLOGSPOT.COM

Robbie pastors the Mission Church of the Nazarene, a church she and her husband, Mac, planted in Hammond, Indiana. Robbie preaches with gusto, passion, and a rich theological savviness. She stands among the rare female church planters in our day, and she's leading with grace and love.

CHRISTINE CAINE

CHRISTINECAINE.COM

Christine Caine is an internationally known pastor at Hillsong Church in Australia. She is a powerful Bible teacher to both men and women. Christine has a passion for justice, and with her husband she founded the anti–human trafficking organization the A21 Campaign. Christine also founded Propel Women, which is an organization to inspire and equip women in line with their passions.

NOEMI CHAVEZ

7THSTREETCHURCH.COM

Noemi Chavez is a colaborer and lead pastor with her husband, Joshua Chavez. Together, they lead Seventh Street Church in Long Beach, California. Noemi's preaching podcasts are passionate, edifying, dynamic, challenging, and relational.

TRACEY BIANCHI

TRACEYBIANCHI.COM

Tracey is an innovative teaching pastor at Christ Church of Oak Brook, a fast-growing megachurch in the western suburbs of Chicago. Next to Senior Pastor Dan Meyer, Tracey preaches challenging and relevant messages on weekends. In 2009, a new worship service was launched under Tracey's visionary leadership, and is today one of the fastest-growing services in the church. Tracey is also an author, a speaker, and a fierce hockey player.

A PROFILE AN EMBOLDENED CHURCH

SEATTLEQUEST.ORG

Quest Church is one of the most beautiful pictures of an emboldened church. Although it is mostly known for its gifted pastor, Eugene Cho, Quest is staffed with male and female pastors from a rainbow of cultures. The platform is always diverse on Sunday mornings, and both men and women preach on a regular basis. Eugene Cho writes and speaks for women on a regular basis, teaching on the full inclusion of women in leadership. Quest Church is totally committed to the gospel, and models what it looks like to be on mission with diverse voices leading the way.

THIS IS OUR STORY

This is our story. We are emboldened women and men, partnering together, and riding the wave of the Spirit. Now is our time, dear church. Not tomorrow, but now. Now is the time for women to claim their full callings and be freed from gender-based restrictions. Now is the time for women to rise up and use their God-given gifts with boldness. Now is the time for the church to no longer be lopsided, but to move forward in its full potential, with men and women serving alongside one another—unhindered. Now is the time to be the church we were always meant to be—a sign and wonder.

Dear brothers and sisters in Christ, and emboldened church, hear these words: I need your preaching, teaching, and leading, and you need mine. I need to break bread with you, and you need to break bread with me. I need your conversation, and you need mine. I need you in my life and you need me in yours. I need a seat at the table, and so do you. You don't have to do this alone. You can't. Not if you we are going to be an emboldened church on this kingdom mission. I need you, you need me, we need you, and you need us. Together—arm in arm—we are an emboldened church, just as we were designed to be.

I leave you with these powerful words from the apostle Paul:

> May the Lord make your love increase and overflow for each other and for everyone else, just as ours does for you. May he strengthen your hearts so that you will be blameless and holy in the presence of our God and Father when our Lord Jesus comes with all his holy ones. (1 Thess 3:12-14)

ACKNOWLEDGMENTS

SOMETIMES IDEAS ARE BIRTHED over a lifetime, and sometimes in an instant. *Emboldened* is both. While the narrative and teachings of this book have been formed throughout my journey in ministry, the idea came during a lunch with Mandy Smith and Al Hsu. I'm not sure I would have been so bold to approach an editor without the pushing and prompting of Mandy Smith. Mandy, thank you for giving me such a clear vision for women serving the bride of Christ. Thank you for emboldening me. Thank you, Scot McKnight, for coming alongside me all of these years as a mentor, friend, teacher, and encourager. You have infused more confidence and wisdom in my life than I could ever ask for. Thank you for reading my manuscript over and over again. Thank you to the many who read my manuscript and offered invaluable feedback, including Brandon Edgbert, Melody Rensberger, Larry Rench, and Sharon Soper. Thank you, Kim Thomas, for the countless messages of encouragement to keep going, and Stacey Maljian for keeping me grounded and humble. Thank you, Mom, Dad, Stu, and Lynn, for the countless times you took the boys so I could sneak in some writing time. Thank you, PazNaz, for allowing me to be your shepherd and for living into this kingdom vision of Jesus. I love you more than you know. Finally, thank you Jeff, Caleb, and Noah. You are the loves of my life. Jeff, you live the cruciform life of Jesus more than anyone I know. Caleb and Noah, I pray that you bravely live the emboldened life for Jesus daily. I love you.

APPENDIX

Books to Read

Cohick, Lynn. *Women in the World of the Earliest Christians: Illuminating Ancient Ways of Life*. Grand Rapids: Baker Academic, 2009.

James, Carolyn Custis. *Half the Church: Recapturing God's Global Vision for Women*. Grand Rapids: Zondervan, 2011.

McKnight, Scot. *The Blue Parakeet: Rethinking How You Read the Bible*. Grand Rapids: Zondervan, 2010.

———. *Junia Is Not Alone*. Englewood, CO: Patheos Press, 2011.

Pierce, Ronald W., and Rebecca Merrill Groothuis, eds. *Discovering Biblical Equality: Complementarity Without Hierarchy*. Downers Grove, IL: IVP Academic, 2005.

Stackhouse, John G., Jr. *Finally Feminist: a Pragmatic Christian Understanding of Gender*. Grand Rapids: Baker Academic, 2005.

Webb, William J. *Slaves, Women and Homosexuals: Exploring the Hermeneutics of Cultural Analysis*. Downers Grove, IL: IVP Academic, 2001.

NOTES

INTRODUCTION: A BURDEN FOR THE CHURCH

[1]"Women in Ministry | Church of the Nazarene Presence in the Great Lakes Megaregion 1900-2014," *Professor Price* (blog), accessed May 18, 2017, www.professorprice.net/blog/women-in-ministry-church-of -the-nazarene-presence-in-the-great-lakes-megaregion-1900-2014.

[2]"Women Clergy Stats 1994-2014," Research Services, Church of the Nazarene Global Ministry Center, August 7, 2015, www.nazarene.org /research-services.

[3]"Christian Women Today, Part 1 of 4: What Women Think of Faith, Leadership and Their Role in Church," Barna, August 13, 2012, www .barna.org/barna-update/culture/579-christian-women-today-part -1-of-4-what-women-think-of-faith-leadership-and-their-role-in -the-church#.Vqkwx_HOUmc].

[4]For some important scholarship on this topic see the appendix, "Books to Read."

1 THIS IS OUR STORY

[1]Parts of this chapter are adapted from Tara Beth Leach, "From Bitter Sorrow to Joyful Expectation," *Tara Beth Leach* (blog), April 5, 2015, http://tarabethleach.com/from-bitter-sorrow-to-joyful-expectation; and Tara Beth Leach, "Dear Pastor, Do You Remember When?," *Tara Beth Leach* (blog), September 30, 2015, http://tarabethleach.com/dear -pastor-do-you-remember-when.

[2]James D. G. Dunn, *Jesus Remembered* (Grand Rapids: Eerdmans, 2003), 832-33.

[3]See Mt 4:23; 26:6-12; 27:55, 61; Mk 14:3-9; 15:40-41; Lk 8:2-3; 12:31; 18:22; 23:49, 55; Jn 11:2; 12:3-8.

[4]Scot McKnight, *Junia Is Not Alone* (Englewood, CO: Patheos Press, 2011), Kindle ed., loc. 55.

[5]Jerome, *Epistle* 127.2-7, as quoted in Ruth A. Tucker and Walter L. Liefeld, *Daughters of the Church: Women and Ministry from New Testament Times to the Present* (Grand Rapids: Zondervan, 1987), 118.

[6]J. M. Cohen, introduction to *Teresa of Ávila, The Life of Saint Teresa of Ávila by Herself*, trans. J. M. Cohen (London: Penguin Classics, 1988), 12.

[7]Ibid., 22.

[8]Mary B. Woodworth-Etter, *Signs and Wonders: God Wrought in the Ministry for Forty Years* (Tulsa: Harrison, 1916), 21.

[9]Ibid., 7.

[10]Patricia Gundry, quoted in Jon Trott, "Woman Be Free! Interview with Patricia Gundry," *Blue Christian on a Red Background*, September 25, 2006, http://bluechristian.blogspot.com/2006/09/woman-be-free-interview-with-patricia.html.

[11]Pamela D. H. Cochran, *Evangelical Feminism: A History* (New York: NYU Press, 2005), 46.

2 OVERCOMING IMPOSTER SYNDROME

[1]*Elf*, directed by John Favreau (Los Angeles: New Line Home Entertainment, 2004).

[2]Sheryl Sandberg, *Lean In: Women, Work, and the Will to Lead* (New York: Knopf, 2013), 29-30.

[3]Ibid., 30.

[4]This and the next paragraph are taken from Tara Beth Leach, "Paris, Suffering, and the Redemptive Community," *Tara Beth Leach* (blog), November 15, 2015, http://tarabethleach.com/paris-suffering-and-the-redemptive-community.

[5]This and the preceding paragraph are adapted from Tara Beth Leach, "When She Preaches," Missio Alliance, October 26, 2015, www.missioalliance.org/when-she-preaches.

[6]Gordon D. Fee, *Paul, the Spirit, and the People of God* (Grand Rapids: Baker Academic, 1996), 146.

[7]Mandy Smith, *The Vulnerable Pastor: How Human Limitations Empower Our Ministry* (Downers Grove, IL: InterVarsity Press, 2015), 11-12.

[8]Jackie Roese, *Lime Green* (Dallas: HIS Publishing, 2015), xiv-xv.

[9]Tara Beth Leach, "I Don't Fit the Senior Pastor Mold," *Christianity Today*, September 12, 2016, www.christianitytoday.com/women -leaders/2016/september/i-dont-fit-senior-pastor-mold.html.

3 BREAKING STEREOTYPES

[1]Parts of this chapter are adapted from Tara Beth Leach, "I Don't Fit the Senior Pastor Mold," *Christianity Today*, September 12, 2016, www.christianitytoday.com/women-leaders/2016/september /i-dont-fit-senior-pastor-mold.html; and Tara Beth Leach, "We Are Feminine (But We Won't Fit in Your Box)," *Tara Beth Leach* (blog), November 11, 2015, http://tarabethleach.com/we-are-feminine-but-we -wont-fit-in-your-box.

[2]Sheryl Sandberg, *Lean In: Women, Work, and the Will to Lead* (New York: Knopf, 2013), 40.

[3]Emma Gray, "Stop Attributing the Success of Women Olympians to Men," *Huffington Post*, August 15, 2016, www.huffingtonpost.com /entry/women-olympians-dont-need-men-to-be-badass_us_57a 87489e4b03ba68012ccbb.

[4]Ibid.

[5]Sandberg, *Lean In*, 41.

[6]Jackie Roese, *She Can Teach: Empowering Women to Teach the Scriptures Effectively* (Eugene, OR: Wipf & Stock, 2013), 9.

[7]Scot McKnight, *The Blue Parakeet: Rethinking How You Read the Bible* (Grand Rapids: Zondervan, 2010), 168-69.

[8]Ibid., 167.

4 OVERCOMING OPPOSITION

[1]Portions of this chapter are adapted from Tara Beth Leach, "Women, Keep On Preaching On," *Tara Beth Leach* (blog), July 28, 2015, http://tarabethleach.com/women-keep-on-preaching-on; and Tara Beth Leach, "Hellfire in Heels or Daughters of the Resurrection?," Missio Alliance, July 29, 2015, www.missioalliance.org/hellfire-in -heels-or-daughters-of-the-resurrection.

[2]You will find Jory's blog at www.JoryMicah.com.

[3]Scot McKnight, *The Blue Parakeet: Rethinking How You Read the Bible* (Grand Rapids: Zondervan, 2010).

[4]Adapted from Lee Jay Berman, "13 Tools for Resolving Conflict in the Workplace, with Customers and in Life," Mediate.com, www.mediate .com/articles/bermanlj3.cfm.

5 AN EMBOLDENED SISTERHOOD

[1]Stephanie K. Johnson, David R. Hekman, and Elsa T. Chan, "If There's Only One Woman in Your Candidate Pool, There's Statistically No Chance She'll Be Hired," *Harvard Business Review*, April 26, 2016, https:// hbr.org/2016/04/if-theres-only-one-woman-in-your-candidate -pool-theres-statistically-no-chance-shell-be-hired.

[2]Sheryl Sandberg, *Lean In: Women, Work, and the Will to Lead* (New York: Knopf, 2013), 163.

[3]Natasha Sistrunk Robinson, "Hope for More Diverse Conference Lineups," *Christianity Today*, November 2014, www.christianitytoday .com/women/2014/november/hope-for-more-diverse-conference -lineups.html.

[4]Nancy Beach, *Gifted to Lead: the Art of Leading as a Woman in the Church* (Grand Rapids: Zondervan, 2008), 155.

[5]Irene Liguori, "'Mean Girls' Syndrome Studied," *UB Reporter*, May 5, 2005, www.buffalo.edu/ubreporter/archive/vol36/vol36n32/articles /Ostrov.html.

[6]Sarah Bessey, *Jesus Feminist: An Invitation to Revisit the Bible's View of Women* (Nashville: Howard Books, 2013), 125.

[7]Ibid., 132.

6 MARRIAGE, FAMILY, AND SINGLENESS IN MINISTRY

[1]Portions of this chapter are adapted from Tara Beth Leach, "Husbands, Submit to Your Wives," *Christian Week*, October 24, 2016, www.chris tianweek.org/husbands-submit-wives; and Tara Beth Leach, "Hus-bands, Submit to Your Wives," *Missio Alliance*, June 24, 2015, www.missioalliance.org/husbands-submit-to-your-wives.

[2]*Egalitarianism* means "equal" or "level," and teaches that Christians are created equally in God's sight and also have equal roles in the body of Christ and in marriage. Complementarians believe that men and women are created equal but have different roles within marriage and in the body of Christ. Men are in the place of leadership and authority, while women have a supporting role.

[3]Scot McKnight, *The Blue Parakeet: Rethinking How You Read the Bible* (Grand Rapids: Zondervan, 2010), 197.

[4]Ibid.

[5]Ibid., 164.

[6]Sheryl Sandberg, *Lean In: Women, Work, and the Will to Lead* (New York: Knopf, 2013), 122.

[7]Ibid., 123.

[8]Lore Ferguson, "Why Singles Belong in Church Leadership," *Christianity Today*, July 2014, www.christianitytoday.com/women/2014/july /why-singles-belong-in-church-leadership.html.

[9]Amanda Berry Smith, quoted in *African American Religious History: A Documentary Witness*, ed. Milton C. Sernett, 2nd ed. (Durham, NC: Duke University Press Books, 2000), 275.

7 AN EMBOLDENED MISSION

[1]Christopher J. H. Wright, *The Mission of God: Unlocking the Bible's Grand Narrative* (Downers Grove, IL: IVP Academic, 2006), 67.

[2]Kate Shellnutt, "How Single Women Became an Unstoppable Force in Bible Translation," *Christianity Today*, April 2017, www.christianity today.com/women/2017/april/how-single-women-became-unstop pable-force-in-bible-translat.html.

[3]Ibid.

[4]Monica Hardy, quoted in Vashti M. McKenzie, *Not Without a Struggle: Leadership for African American Women in Ministry*, 2nd ed. (Cleveland, OH: Pilgrim Press, 2011), 151.

[5]Ibid., 151-52; emphasis added.

8 AN EMBOLDENED IMAGINATION

[1]Portions of this chapter are adapted from Tara Beth Leach, "When She Preaches," Missio Alliance, October 26, 2015, www.missioalliance.org /when-she-preaches.

[2]Scot McKnight, *Junia Is Not Alone* (Englewood, CO: Patheos Press, 2011), appendix 6.

9 EMBOLDENED COLABORERS

[1]Portions of this chapter are adapted from Tara Beth Leach, "Dear Bill Hybels and Other Men Who Affirm Women in Ministry," Missio

Alliance, August 10, 2015, www.missioalliance.org/dear-bill-hybels
-and-other-men-who-affirm-women-in-ministry.

[2]Halee Gray Scott, *Dare Mighty Things: Mapping the Challenges of Leadership for Christian Women* (Grand Rapids: Zondervan, 2014), 185.

[3]Ibid., 186.

[4]Ibid.

[5]Bill Hybels, Global Leadership Summit, Willow Creek Community Church, Barrington, IL, August 2015.

[6]Ibid.

[7]JR. Forasteros, "Four Ways Men Can Support Women in Ministry," in *Jory Micah* (blog), March 11, 2016, www.jorymicah.com/four-ways-men-can-support-women-in-ministry-by-jr-forasteros.

10 AN EMBOLDENED CHURCH

[1]Parts of this chapter are adapted from Tara Beth Leach, "Becoming #TrulyHuman . . . Together," Missio Alliance, March 23, 2015, www.missioalliance.org/becoming-trulyhuman-together.

[2]Ruth Tucker, *Daughters of the Church* (Grand Rapids: Zondervan, 1987), 273.

[3]Frances Willard, quoted in ibid., 274.

[4]Ibid.

[5]Tara Beth Leach, "The Symphonic Melody: Wesleyan Holiness Theology Meets New Perspective Paul," in *The Apostle Paul and the Christian Life: Ethical and Missional Implications of the New* Perspective, ed. Scot McKnight and Joe Modica (Grand Rapids: Baker Academic 2016), 165-66.

[6]Patriarchy is not a prescriptive model for the church to live by; rather, it is descriptive and a backdrop to the Old Testament's story. For more on this see Carolyn Custis James, *Malestrom: Manhood Swept into the Currents of a Changing World* (Grand Rapids: Zondervan, 2015).

ABOUT THE AUTHOR

TARA BETH LEACH is the senior pastor at First Church of the Nazarene of Pasadena (PazNaz) in Southern California. She is a graduate of Olivet Nazarene University (BA, youth ministry) and Northern Theological Seminary (MDiv). A regular writer for Missio Alliance, she has also contributed to other publications such as *Christianity Today*,  *Christian Week*, *Jesus Creed*, *The Table* magazine, *Reflecting the Image* devotional, and *Renovating Holiness*. Most recently she contributed a chapter, "The Symphonic Melody: Wesleyan Holiness Theology Meets New Perspective Paul," in *The Apostle Paul and the Christian Life: Ethical and Missional Implications of the New Perspective*, ed. Scot McKnight and Joseph B. Modica (Baker Academic, 2016). Tara Beth is also the author of *Kingdom Culture* (Beacon Hill Press, 2017). She has two beautiful and rambunctious children, Caleb and Noah, and has been married to the love of her life, Jeff, since 2006.

Social Media
Use #Emboldened to join in on the conversation!

Follow Tara Beth Leach
TaraBethLeach.com
Facebook.com/TaraBethLeachAuthor
Instagram: TaraBeth82
Twitter: TaraBeth82
Email: TaraBeth82@gmail.com

Missio Alliance

Missio Alliance has arisen in response to the shared voice of pastors and ministry leaders from across the landscape of North American Christianity for a new "space" of togetherness and reflection amid the issues and challenges facing the church in our day. We are united by a desire for a fresh expression of evangelical faith, one significantly informed by the global evangelical family. Lausanne's Cape Town Commitment, "A Confession of Faith and a Call to Action," provides an excellent guidepost for our ethos and aims.

Through partnerships with schools, denominational bodies, ministry organizations, and networks of churches and leaders, Missio Alliance addresses the most vital theological and cultural issues facing the North American Church in God's mission today. We do this primarily by convening gatherings, curating resources, and catalyzing innovation in leadership formation.

Rooted in the core convictions of evangelical orthodoxy, the ministry of Missio Alliance is animated by a strong and distinctive theological identity that emphasizes

Comprehensive Mutuality: Advancing the partnered voice and leadership of women and men among the beautiful diversity of the body of Christ across the lines of race, culture, and theological heritage.

Hopeful Witness: Advancing a way of being the people of God in the world that reflects an unwavering and joyful hope in the lordship of Christ in the church and over all things.

Church in Mission: Advancing a vision of the local church in which our identity and the power of our testimony is found and expressed through our active participation in God's mission in the world.

In partnership with InterVarsity Press, we are pleased to offer a line of resources authored by a diverse range of theological practitioners. The resources in this series are selected based on the important way in which they address and embody these values, and thus, the unique contribution they offer in equipping Christian leaders for fuller and more faithful participation in God's mission.

missioalliance.org | twitter.com/missioalliance | facebook.com/missioalliance

More Titles from
InterVarsity Press and Missio Alliance

The Church as Movement
978-0-8308-4133-2

Embrace
978-0-8308-4471-5

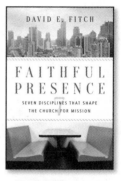

Faithful Presence
978-0-8308-4127-1

Paradoxology
978-0-8308-4504-0

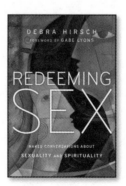

Redeeming Sex
978-0-8308-3639-0

White Awake
978-0-8308-4393-0

Please visit us at ivpress.com.